Let's Connect!

DM me on Instagram with any questions - I promise, I'll answer ☺

Let's get started!

@Chelsea.Peitz

CONTENTS

SECTION THREE: BUILD YOUR REACH

SECTION FOUR: BUILD YOUR RESOURCES

INTRODUCTION

You bought this book to learn what to post and how to make it matter to your customers.

You want to learn how to create content that gets engagement and ultimately builds brand awareness, creates community and generates business.

In order to do that, you need to first:

- Understand what a personal brand is and what components we control and don't
- Get clear about who specifically you want to reach with your content
- Define your core values and be able to articulate them in simple jargon free terms

Once you've completed those steps, you'll have the foundation you need to create valuable and relevant content consistently and stress free.

This workbook is broken down into four sections:

1. Build your brand
2. Build your content
3. Build your reach
4. Build your resources

In case you're wondering, I've been in the real estate industry for over 20 years. I got my license in 2001 **B. F.** [that's Before Facebook] which means I earned my living as a Realtor® without ever using social media, mainly because it didn't exist.

I didn't grow up with the Internet of Things nor am I a digital native and I graduated college before Y2K which means, regardless of your generation or age, you too can adapt, evolve and master social media.

While I'm no longer a practicing agent, I've continued to work within the real estate niche teaching thousands of agents, loan officers and title sales executives how to harness the power of social media to create a powerful personal brand and generate FREE business.

My goal is to make content creation easy with my step-by-step formulas and templates that leave you NO excuse but to experience massive success!

Let's get started!

Stop Complicating Content - *Let's make this easy and straight to the point*

AMPLIFY YOUR CONTENT WITH A CLEARLY DEFINED BRAND

———

"You have to be a brand to be relevant today, the world has changed. Anyone with a smartphone is now a journalist, you have computers writing articles. How are you and I going to stay relevant today? How is anyone going to stay relevant today – it's your brand."

Mark Schaefer, Author & Social Media Expert

WHAT IS A BRAND?

———

What does a personal brand have to do with content – everything!

In today's "reputation economy" it's critical to create a brand that can be easily Googled. We make decisions based on star ratings and friends in common and wonder what's wrong when we DON'T see your brand on The Socials.

We now build trust through technology which means that today's consumer expects to find your brand (and it's content) with one click, swipe or scroll.

Consumers will stalk your Socials before or after connecting with you simply because they can. Viewing your posts, blogs and YouTube videos will likely impact whether they will like you, trust you and want to work with you.

Content is the foundation of your personal brand and through today's most powerful distribution channel in the world, social media, you share it with your audience. Your social media posts may be the first experience a potential customer has with your brand. It can also be the reason that someone decides to reach out and become a client.

BEFORE YOU CAN CREATE HIGHLY RELEVANT CUSTOMER FOCUSED CONTENT YOU MUST DEFINE:

- Your brand values and voice
- How your expertise, product or service uniquely solves your customer's problems
- What differentiates you from the competition
- What niche you desire to serve
- Your ideal customer's challenges and goals
- Your industry's positive and negative disruptive trends

The following sections outline the pathway to building a powerful personal brand

PATHWAY TO A POWERFUL PERSONAL BRAND

NICHE |UVP

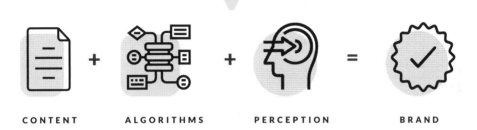

CONTENT   +   ALGORITHMS   +   PERCEPTION   =   BRAND

CONTENT:
WE DO CONTROL

We create the content and decide through which platforms to distribute that content and at what frequency.

ALGORITHMS:
WE DON'T CONTROL

In very basic terms, an algorithm is a set of instructions designed to perform a specific task. A recipe is a kind of algorithm. The recipe has instructions that tells you what to do in steps. It takes inputs (ingredients) and produces an output (the completed dish)

The Socials all have algorithms made up of hundreds of thousands of inputs that lead to different outputs. This inputs in this case are your behaviors (the content you like and the posts you engage with) that then produces an output (the posts placed into your feed).

While we don't know all of the ingredients in Facebook or Instagram's secret recipe, we can leverage what we do know to create a successful post.

PERCEPTION:
WE SEMI CONTROL

When I refer to "perception," I'm talking about the customer's perception of your brand that is created by how often they see and experience your brand online, in the feed or in their email inbox.

STEP 1

(Step one is about figuring out your UVP and Identifying your niche customer)

**IDENTIFY UNIQUE
VALUE PROPOSITION** ·············> **IDENTIFY
NICHE**

STEP 2

(Once you have that down, move into step 2 which is about creating the content
that showcases your UVP and solves your ideal customer's challenge)

+

CREATE CONTENT

Pick idea/theme

CONTEXT

The meaning of the message delivered
to the right people at the right time

5 E'S	FORMAT	ENGAGE
Educational	Video	Comments
Entertaining	Photo	Shout Outs
Engaging	Audio	Direct Messages
Emotional	Written	
Exclusive		

DISTRIBUTION

BUILD PHASE
CONSISTENCY
- Doesn't mean daily
- Sets up expectations

GROW PHASE
FREQUENCY
- Accelerates growth

+

STEP 3

(Step 3 is then how you need to work with algorithms and understand how to
leverage them to get your content and your brand out there)

ALGORITHMS

ENGAGEMENT   **REACH**

♥ **TRUST**

ACTIVATE YOUR POWERFUL PERSONAL BRAND

"Personal branding is about managing your name—even if you don't own a business—in a world of misinformation, disinformation, and semi-permanent Google records. Going on a date? Chances are that your "blind" date has Googled your name. Going to a job interview? Ditto."

Tim Ferriss, Author & Podcaster

CREATE YOUR POWERFUL PERSONAL BRAND

Clarify your brand by answering these thought provoking questions:

WHAT BRINGS YOU JOY?

What are 3-5 topics that you are most passionate about? (does not need to be related to business)

PEOPLE ALWAYS ASK ME ABOUT...

- *What do you know more about that most others?*
- *Can you lean into those areas of expertise and incorporate them into your current role?*

WHAT ARE 2-3 THINGS THAT PEOPLE ARE ALWAYS SURPRISED OR DELIGHTED TO LEARN ABOUT YOU?

Surprising talents? Awards? Accomplishments?
Can you incorporate or combine any of these into your professional brand?

For example: You're a certified pilot - can you connect the talents used in flying to your current professional role?

WHAT IS YOUR #1 "SUPERPOWER"?

The thing that you do better than anyone else!
- *What feels easy to you that's hard for others?*
- *What are you doing when you feel the most confident?*

For example: I make hard things really easy to understand or I am really skilled at coming up with new ideas quickly, or People love my personality and always feel like they can trust me

3 WORDS THAT DESCRIBE YOU?

Create your own list and then ask a co-worker/friend/significant other what words they would use!

WHAT ARE YOUR BIGGEST WEAKNESSES?

Weakness ·····························> *Turn into a STRENGTH*

WHAT ARE MY NON-NEGOTIABLES?

Can you leverage these into your core values? Are these also your strengths?

For example: dishonesty, disloyalty etc

PAST CAREERS

What unique projects did you work on or what expertise did you gain in the past that can be applied to your current work?

WHAT "BAD HABITS" ARE IMPACTING YOUR PRODUCTIVITY?

Watching TV? Scrolling on Social? What will you put in place to ensure not getting distracted by them?

WHAT IS YOUR PERSONALITY TYPE?

Knowing your personality type helps you communicate effectively with others and understand which situations will help you perform at your best.

Check out these free online style tests:
www.16personalities.com/free-personality-test
www.123test.com/disc-profiles

WHO'S PERSONAL BRAND DO YOU ADMIRE?

What about their brand do you admire?

WHO CAN YOU ALIGN WITH, MEET WITH OR CREATE A MENTORSHIP WITH?

What will YOU offer to that person? Make a list and commit to connecting with them online and in person. Can you promote their content efforts? Can you make introductions and connect dots virtually and in person?

WHAT SCARES YOU THE MOST ABOUT MAKING CONTENT? ABOUT SOCIAL MEDIA? ABOUT MARKETING OR SALES?

Not knowing what to say? Your on-camera presence?

WHAT KIND OF CONTENT FORMAT DO YOU PREFER?

To create? To consume? (written, audio, video?)

"We're not selling bricks. We're selling imagination."
Lars Silberbauer, Global Senior Director of Social Media
and Video, LEGO

WHAT ARE YOU REALLY SELLING? WHAT PROBLEM DO YOU SPECIFICALLY SOLVE?

Hint: it's not your product or service

WHAT DO YOU GET IN RETURN WHEN YOU SOLVE THOSE PROBLEMS?

Prestige? Influence? Status? More security for family?

WHAT ARE 1-3 SHORT TERM AND 1-3 FUNDAMENTAL TRENDS IMPACTING YOUR INDUSTRY IN THE NEXT 10 YEARS POSITIVELY, NEGATIVELY OR BOTH?

How will they change the normal course of business? What can you or your company do to support your customers for both?

Examples for inspiration
- iBuyers
- Artificial intelligence
- Blockchain
- Commission compression

WHAT ARE THE ASSUMPTIONS THAT THE CONSUMER OR YOUR CUSTOMER BASE MAKE ABOUT YOUR ROLE/SERVICE?

Outline the positives and negatives. For the negatives, how can you change those?

WHAT IS YOUR CLOSEST COMPETITOR OFFERING THAT YOU ARE NOT?

If you offer the exact same services, what can you create to make you stand out? Why are you not currently offering this service/product?

WHAT ARE SOME QUESTIONS THAT PEOPLE SHOULD BE ASKING YOU, BUT AREN'T?

In other words, they are focused on "X" but should be focused on "Y"

WHAT ARE THE NEEDS YOUR CUSTOMERS CONTINUE TO DISCUSS WITH YOU?

What are the most common questions your customers ask?

Review your emails, text messages, direct messages and calls for insights.

ARE YOU REGULARLY PARTICIPATING IN INDUSTRY NETWORKING EVENTS, MASTERMINDS OR CONFERENCES?

If you already participate in these, can you create and lead your own?

HOW ARE THINGS DONE IN YOUR INDUSTRY, COMPANY OR PERSONAL BUSINESS PLAN?

What would it look like if the way things have been done were the complete opposite tomorrow?

WHAT ARE YOUR 3 MOST SUCCESSFUL METHODS OF GAINING NEW BUSINESS?

Can you change or modify all three? How so? Can you eliminate them and make 3 new ones?

HAVE YOU INTERVIEWED YOUR BEST CLIENTS AND IDENTIFIED THEIR BEST PRACTICES?

Can you compile those into a list or template to share with future clients/prospects?

WHAT ARE THE TOP CHALLENGES FOR A NEW PERSON IN YOUR INDUSTRY?

Can you create a step by step framework for success for both?

TO WHAT OR WHOM DO YOU LISTEN, READ OR WATCH THAT INSPIRES YOU?

Are there specific pieces of content that have inspired you or changed the way you look at your business? What are they and why did they change your perspective?

WHAT DO YOU WANT TO LEARN MORE ABOUT THAT COULD HELP YOU IN YOUR SPECIFIC BUSINESS OR YOUR NICHE CUSTOMERS?

Focus on skills that can help YOU and your customer's business goals. Create this list and research books, courses and events to help you achieve them.

Examples
- Social Media Advertising
- Email Marketing
- Public Speaking
- Video Marketing

IDENTIFY 5 CORE VALUES:

Adaptability	Honesty	Open-Minded	Unflappable
Boldness	Ingenuity	Perceptive	Vision
Compassion	Just	Quality of work	Wonder
Dependability	Knowledgeable	Results-oriented	Yes-minded
Ethical	Leadership	Selfless	Zest
Fortitude	Mindful	Trustworthy	
Growth-minded	Nimble		

Write additional
words here

_____

_____

_____

_____

_____

Core Value List Credit: scottjeffrey.com/core-values-list/

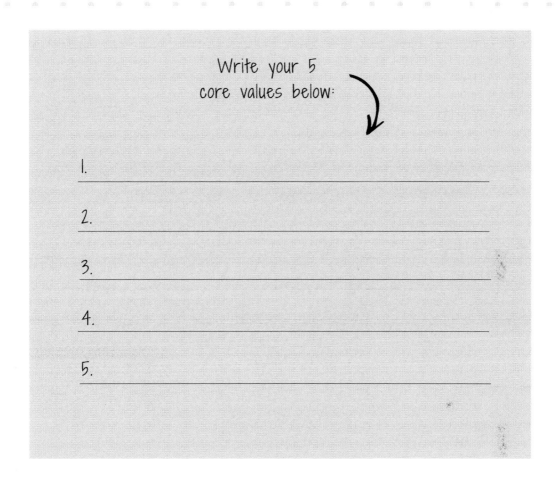

Write your 5
core values below:

1. _____

2. _____

3. _____

4. _____

5. _____

Check out these additional resources for more ideas:

https://corevalueslist.com/

https://contentsparks.com/16896/free-download-big-list-of-core-value-words/

https://scottjeffrey.com/core-values-list/

https://jamesclear.com/core-values

ARTICULATE YOUR UNIQUE VALUE PROPOSITION

"No matter how great your product or service is, nobody will be willing to buy it unless you give them a good reason. The first look an online customer gets at how you can add value to their lives is your Unique Value Proposition."

Campaigncreators.com

WWW.CHELSEAPEITZ.COM

WHAT IS A UNIQUE VALUE PROPOSITION (UVP)?

A Unique Value Proposition, or UVP, is a simple, one sentence statement that identifies who you work with, what value you provide and HOW that impacts your customer.

Why do you need one?
A UVP differentiates you from the competition and provides you with the clarity you need to create content that connects with your ideal audience. Your UVP makes you and your content relevant to the consumer you want to serve.

Your UVP becomes the foundation for all of your content - social media posts, email and website copy. It becomes the heart of your business motivations and empowers you to share WHY someone should work with you over someone else.

When you know who you are and what specific value you provide you can create content that exemplifies these points.

UVP GUIDELINES:

A UVP is NOT a slogan, tagline or catchphrase. It is not a multi-paragraph mission statement. This section will help you develop your own one sentence UVP. Give yourself permission to take on this challenge with an open mind, understanding that your UVP may take weeks or months to evolve as you refine, edit and tweak it.

- One sentence (short and sweet)
- Specific (riches in niches)
- Easy to understand (jargon & industry-lingo free)

- Memorable & repeatable
- Identifies your ideal customer
- What benefits your service provides

THE UVP FORMULA

I DO
WHAT

+

FOR
WHOM

=

THAT
RESULTS IN

HERE'S A FEW OF MY OWN UVPS:

For whom

I do what

Results in

"I share real estate marketing tips that help you grow your business
and make more money doing what you love."

For whom

I do what

"I teach mortgage professionals how to use the camera on their smartphone
to build a powerful personal brand"

Results in

For whom

I do what

"I help title professionals leverage free social media platforms to
increase marketshare and mindshare."

Results in

QUESTIONS TO HELP YOU GET STARTED

- Do you offer extreme specialization or serve an ultra-niche?
- Do you have incredible results for ecstatic clients?
- Do you have a unique customer experience? Marketing method?
- Do you have a compelling background story?
- Do you have complimentary expertise (luxury homes and an expert in horse property?)
- Do you have a unique guarantee?
- Do you have specialized skills from another industry that enhances your current role?
- Have you endured a major pivot in your life?

POSITIVE ACTION VERBS TO USE IN YOUR UVP:

Empower	Cheer	Impact	Produce
Share	Connect	Inspire	Propose
Teach	Delight	Invent	Respond
Help	Deliver	Launch	Revamp
Activate	Demonstrate	Leverage	Train
Adapt	Design	Map	Accelerate
Advance	Engineer	Motivate	Sprint
Amplify	Excite	Navigate	Support
Boost	Execute	Organize	Eliminate
Build	Explain	Overhaul	Expedite
Cause	Generate	Plan	Reduce
Challenge	Go Guide	Present	Streamline

Additional lists of verbs: *https://boompositive.com/pages/list-of-positive-verbs-a-to-z*

FORMULA:

I DO WHAT:

+

FOR WHOM:

=

THAT RESULTS IN:

ATTRACT YOUR IDEAL CUSTOMER

"Imagine your customer is a hitchhiker. You pull over to give him a ride, and the one burning question on his mind is simply Where are you going? But as he approaches, you roll down the window and start talking about your mission statement, or how your grandfather built this car with his bare hands, or how your road-trip playlist is all 1980s alternative. This person doesn't care."

Donald Miller - Author, Building a StoryBrand

IDENTIFY YOUR IDEAL CUSTOMER

Building a Customer Avatar

An avatar is simply a profile of your ideal customer. The profile should be very detailed and include specifics about one person to help you identify their specific needs which will, in turn, help you create content that can fulfill those needs and speaks directly to their pain points and personality style.

Your goal is to envision a specific customer and learn their motivations, challenges, likes and dislikes. Without knowing who you are talking to or trying to reach, knowing what to post is unclear.

Answer the below questions in as much detail as possible.

BACKGROUND INFO AND DEMOGRAPHICS

Age, Gender, Occupation, Income, Parent, Pet Owner, City, Suburbs

PREFERRED METHOD OF COMMUNICATION

Phone, Text, Email, Direct Message

PERSONALITY STYLE

Detail oriented, Analytical, Introvert, Assertive etc

WHY ARE THEY CURRENTLY NOT WORKING WITH YOU?

They are not aware of you/They work with a competitor/Other

WHAT IS YOUR CUSTOMER AFRAID OF?

Making the wrong decision? Losing money? Not getting a good deal?

Most important of all!

WHAT ARE THEIR PAIN POINTS?

For example: Finding a home in the right school district or working with a trustworthy advisor

WHAT ARE THEIR BUSINESS/FINANCIAL GOALS?

For example: Affordability and down payment, creating wealth through real estate or first time home buyer – making the best decisions

WHY IS THIS PERSON YOUR IDEAL CUSTOMER?

WHAT REALLY MATTERS TO THEIR WORLD?

WHAT QUESTIONS DO THEY ASK AT THE BEGINNING, MIDDLE AND END OF THE PROCESS?

Blake Thompson

Founder, Marketing Inc. start up

ABOUT

Income: $150-200k/yr

Age: 34

Single/Married: Engaged

Children/Pets: 1 senior chihuahua, no kids but plans to start family within 3 years

Communication Style: Text message, social direct message and phone for detailed discussions (more efficient and fast in some cases)

Preferred social media: Instagram, Facebook, LinkedIn

Personality Style: Bullet point information; doesn't like to waste time or fluff – get to the point he's busy and often traveling for work; likes to receive an update daily

Hobbies: Training for half marathon, brunch with friends, wine tasting

BLAKE'S STORY

Blake is relocating to the city of Chicago and prefers an urban, downtown vibe with a family friendly neighborhood. His fiancé leans towards a traditional single family style property that feels more "home-y" while Blake loves modern clean lines in a high rise.

Blake has bought one home previously which he is keeping as a rental and he is now self-employed. Blake is afraid of overpaying for a home in his desired area and not finding a home with enough room to grow into. He's also stressed about finding a mortgage professional and property

manager that can assist him with his qualifying and rental needs.

They also don't want the headache of fully remodeling an older property but could consider this option for the right location and right price.

PAIN POINTS/CHALLENGES

- His major challenge is finding something in the city with enough space for 3 bedrooms and has an easy commute to the airport due to his high volume travel but with enough charm for his soon to be wife and that's within budget.

- Totally new to the area – learning what neighborhoods best fit their needs

- Feels empowered by technology and real estate search sites but isn't sure how much negotiating power he has as a buyer in a hot market

- Inventory for high rise condos with more than 2 beds within his price range are few and far between, he will need to rely on an expert to help him seek out and find options

- Bidding wars require top notch negotiations in a low inventory marketplace

- Understanding the ins and outs of qualifying as an entrepreneur

- Managing a rental property and how that impacts a new loan

- Managing a rental property in another state

CONNECT WITH CONTENT (THE 5 E'S)

"Content is King,
but context is God."

Gary Vaynerchuk, Author & Speaker

THE 5 E'S OF CONTENT
The Context Commandments

———

Now that you know who you're talking to and what value you provide, it's time to start making quality content.

The goal of your content should be to provide value to the consumer, positively promote your brand and create conversations that generate leads.

So, how do you make "good" content that doesn't get scrolled or swiped past?

By adding *Context*.

So what exactly is the difference between content and context?

> *"Content is the material/matter/medium contained within the work that's available for audience. Context is the positioning of the content, storyline or purpose that provides value to the audience."*
> Erin Ashley Simon

In basic terms, context is how you give your content meaning. It describes the purpose of your content to the audience and it's what connects that message to the consumers head and their heart.

Context is what keeps your content relevant to a specific industry, niche or customer- it sets the purpose and impacts the outcome of your content.

Context IS the value of the content.

Value comes in all shapes and sizes. You don't have to exclusively teach something to provide value. Making someone laugh, feel heard or supported is also providing value. Asking for help or advice gives value to the recipient but also allows the advice-giver to feel valued.

You can improve your context by asking for feedback, listening to your community and executing on their input. By consistently fulfilling a consumer's content needs you will ultimately build your brand's credibility which leads to trust.

Lastly, and perhaps most importantly, your support of others' content through your comments provides massive value.

Let your comments become your content.

Here's more on the concept of context

Marketing Guru, Gary Vaynerchuk (Gary Vee) speaks about the importance of creating relevant content with the right context

GARY VEE'S GOLDEN RULES OF CONTEXT

- Provide value to the consumer without a sales pitch
- Create content in an appropriate format for the platform
- Don't force someone to sit through an ad to consume it
- Post consistently to build brand visibility and reliability
- Do what you excel at – if you write well create a blog, if you like video, do that

- Spend time where your clients are
- Engage proactively and reactively
- Forget about what you think matters and start making what the consumer cares about
- Read comments, start listening to feedback and execute based on those insights

www.garyvaynerchuk.com/content-is-king-but-context-is-god/)

*Use the "5 E's" guide to help you create content with context,
that provides value and generates engagement*

EDUCATIONAL

Become the resource, build credibility and authority on your niche topic.

"When people have questions about complex or confusing topics, they look for authoritative voices that help explain, illustrate, or enlighten. And when they find an expert opinion on the subject in question, they begin to form a relationship with that content source—perhaps even becoming a future client." – skyword.com

When you strategically share your expertise for free, you show your audience that you are truly a master of your craft. My motto is "teach before you reach" to solidify your reputation and build instant credibility.

Examples

- Explainer or How To videos describing transactional processes of buying or selling a home

- Create helpful community focused content such as: local restaurants where kids eat free, neighborhood activity lists or the step by step process of getting children registered for school in your district complete with teacher/principal interviews after school program info

Facebook Live:
Expert interview and Q&A with Industry Expert Travis Thom

Travis Thom, Elevated Real Estate Marketing
Facebook.com/TheTravisThom

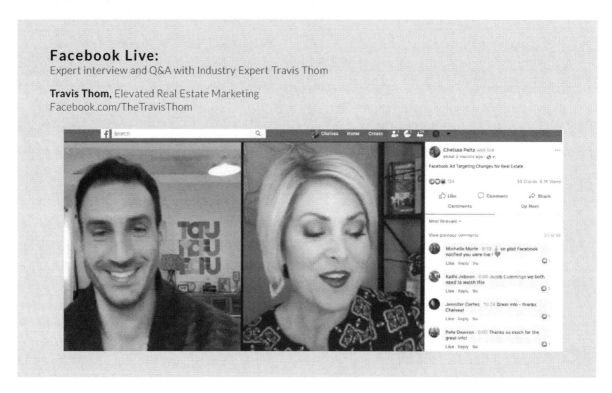

Facebook Vertical Video Post:

15 second video with accompanying text summary (link to article in comments).

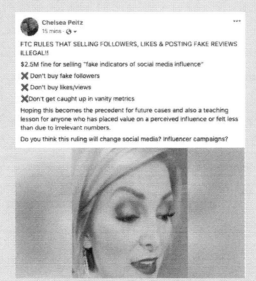

LinkedIn Document Post:

PDF attachment (can also use PPTX or WORD) with accompanying description and tagging of original creator.

Chelsea Peitz
Social Media Coach • Podcaster • Spam-free LinkedIn message sender • …
3mo

Are you ready for #LinkedIn Stories to roll out? Yep, just like Instagram, Facebook and Snapchat Stories!!

In 2018, it was reported that LinkedIn was testing a Stories format. Zuckerberg announced in April of 2019 that he believed the Stories format was the future of Facebook.

Personally, I'm a HUGE fan of the Stories format and have documented the last 1,332 days of my life using this format. Stories have allowed me to build a personal brand, share knowledge for free and engage at scale with an incredible community.

Check out this awesome infographic from Domo, Inc. and see just how much the Stories format DOMINATES posts in the Feed.

[277k Stories VS. 55k photo posts every second of the day]

It's likely just a matter of time until we see Stories here as well 🕙

Would you use them ??

#socialmedia #realestate #marketing #instagram

YouTube Video :

Karin Carr Residential Realtor shares educational (and engaging) tips about living in Savannah.

Karin Carr, Georgia Coast Homes Team Keller Williams Realty
www.YoutubeforAgents.com

Living in Savannah GA - What I LOVE and what I HATE

18K views • 1 year ago • 97%

Average Humidity

In this table, the **Daily** number is the average of humidity readings taken every three hours throughout the day. **Morning** percentages are for 7 am and **Afternoon** measures are for 4 pm local standard time.

Average yearly relative humidity (%)

Average Humidity

In this table, the **Daily** number is the average of humidity readings taken every three hours throughout the day. **Morning** percentages are for 7 am and **Afternoon** measures are for 4 pm local standard time.

Average yearly relative humidity (%)

Daily	Place	Morning	Afternoon
70	Athens	85	52
68	Atlanta	82	52
71	Augusta	87	49
71	Columbus	87	51
71	Macon	87	50
73	Savannah	86	54

Example of Karin inserting helpful graphics into video

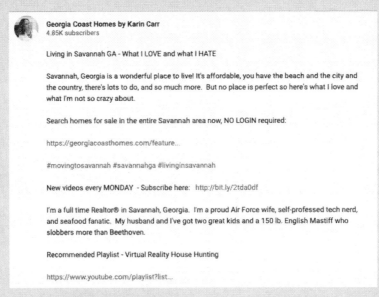

Georgia Coast Homes by Karin Carr
4.85K subscribers

Living in Savannah GA - What I LOVE and what I HATE

Savannah, Georgia is a wonderful place to live! It's affordable, you have the beach and the city and the country, there's lots to do, and so much more. But no place is perfect so here's what I love and what I'm not so crazy about.

Search homes for sale in the entire Savannah area now, NO LOGIN required:

https://georgiacoasthomes.com/feature...

#movingtosavannah #savannahga #livinginsavannah

New videos every MONDAY - Subscribe here: http://bit.ly/2tda0df

I'm a full time Realtor® in Savannah, Georgia. I'm a proud Air Force wife, self-professed tech nerd, and seafood fanatic. My husband and I've got two great kids and a 150 lb. English Mastiff who slobbers more than Beethoven.

Recommended Playlist - Virtual Reality House Hunting

https://www.youtube.com/playlist?list...

YouTube video description:
Karin uses relevant keywords in her title and drives traffic
to sites and video playlists with links.

YouTube Explainer Playlist:

Movement Mortgage's in house marketing team creates short videos based on common client questions.

movement.com

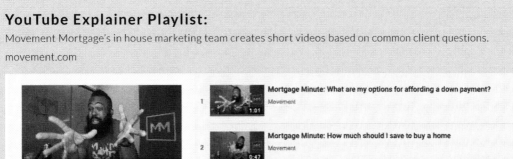

Podcast:

Weekly podcast interviews with industry leaders.

Phil Treadwell, VP of Development Mason-McDuffie Mortgage

industrysyndicate.com/podcasts

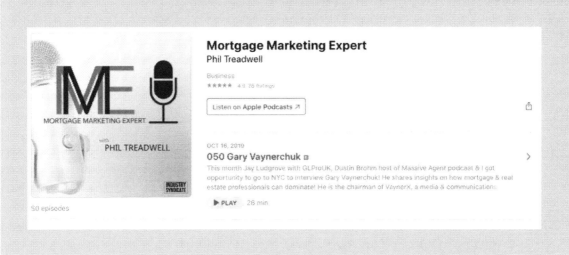

Pinterest Board:

Pinterest Board featuring how to YouTube videos (Pinterest is an excellent web traffic driver!)

Katie Lance, Speaker & Real Estate Coach
katielance.com

@KatieLance How-To Videos

36 Pins · 2,071 followers

Need help on Facebook, Twitter or anything social or tech? This board includes some of my most popular how-to videos. With step-by-step instructions, you won't miss a beat. For more social media tips please visit http://katielance.com or tweet me @katielance!

How to Create Meaningful Engagement | Bring the Online - Offline! | How to Show the Love to Your Clients and Your Community | 5 Quick Tips to Make the Most Out of LinkedIn

IGTV Video Post:

Lizy Hoeffer Irvine shares weekly Money Tips videos for consumers

Lizy Hoeffer Irvine, Chief Experience Officer, Cross Country Mortgage
@lizyirvine

lizyirvine

254 views

lizyirvine 5 Moving Tips To Save You · On average, how much does it cost to move?

Give it a quick google search and you might discover that it's more than you originally anticipated.

Moving expenses can range anywhere from $350 for a one bedroom apartment, to $2,000 for a four-bedroom home -- and that's just for moving services, locally! What about things like packing, packing supplies, unpacking, and new items you'll need in your home?

If you haven't realized by now, the total bill can

IGTV Video Series:

Both Leigh and Justin have created vertical videos for IGTV AND also included them into a "Series" which acts like a Playlist

Leigh Brown, Broker/Owner Leigh Brown & Associates Re/Max Executives
@leighthomasbrown

Justin Konikow, Owner Prime Real Estate Brokerage
@primerealestatebrokerage

Instagram Feed Image Post with Long Form Caption:

chelsea.peitz
Scottsdale, Arizona

chelsea.peitz YIKES!!! Are you making any of these three major hashtag mistakes when you're posting? If so, you could be minimizing your reach and growth!!

📌 BOOKMARK THIS NOW BEFORE YOU FORGET!

1️⃣ Not using enough hashtags (20-30 is goal)

Before you drop the phone, I get it, that's whole lot of hashtags but think of this like playing the lottery - the more tickets you have, the more chances to win

⸺

2️⃣ Not using RELEVANT hashtags that your ideal audience is actively searching for within Instagram

Often times, we think about what industry we're in and come up with hashtags that describe that industry like REALTOR or MORTGAGEPRO, but are those terms that your customer is actually searching?

3️⃣ Not using the right "size" of hashtags or not "layering" different sized hashtags

When I say "size," I mean the number of posts using a specific hashtag. Every hashtag can be searched within Instagram via the Explore tab. After typing in a keyword, simply tap on "Tags" and then select any hashtag of your choice to see the total number of uses, Follow button and posts using that hashtag.

Using only popular hashtags that are used in millions of posts won't help you get seen for very long because so many are using them your post will be buried in seconds!

Instead, use a combination of moderately popular and also smaller niche hashtags for maximum exposure and longevity in the feed!

✦ PS- want your own FREE IG audit!? Just tell me "I want my audit" below!

#iloverealestate #womeninrealestate #socialmediatipsandtricks #realtortips #allthingsrealestate #realestateagent #realtorlife #realestatemarketing #realtormom

Alexa Flash Briefings:
Mini podcasts played through Alexa home device or app

The Real Estate Influencer Buzz
★★★★★ ⌄ 4

FREE
Available instantly on your connected Alexa device.

Supports: English

Daily "buzz" of inspiration, motivation and education for Realtors

Michele "Bee" Bellisari, Residential Realtor, The Bellisari Group at Re/Max Services
#soooboca @themichelebee

The Massive Agent Minute for Real Estate Agents
★★★★★ ⌄ 10

FREE
Available instantly on your connected Alexa device.

Supports: English

Daily Marketing & Business Tips and Inspiration from Dustin Brohm, Host of the Massive Agent Podcast for real estate agents and loan officers

Dustin Brohm, Residential Realtor, EXP Realty
Founder of MassiveAgent.com and Co-Founder IndustrySyndicate.com
MassiveAgent.com

Website Blog Post:

Grant Wise, Real Estate Sales & Lead Gen Coach
MarketingGenius.tv & Witly.com

ENGAGING

Create engagement by asking questions.

Posts that include questions or calls to action generate conversations which can lead to an opportunity for conversion.

Remember – Proactively and intentionally commenting on others' content helps you become the superfan, builds brand and helps the algorithms learn what kinds of content you prefer.

Examples

- Ask for advice or a recommendation
- Ask a "this or that" style of question or take a poll
- Use a poll sticker in your Stories

Facebook Status Update with Text and Color Background:

Chelsea Peitz
October 22 at 10:34 AM · 🌐 ▾

Do you ever dream about the house you grew up in?

⭕⭕ Katie Miller, Alyssa Axelrod and 50 others   106 Comments

LinkedIn Text Post:

Beth Azor, Founder Azor Advisory Services
Commercial Real Estate
Bethazor.com

Beth Azor · 1st
"Canvassing Queen", CRE Leasing
Coach, Developer, Investor, Auth...
2w

I am looking for women....who have personally invested .....in commercial real estate.

Women who took the leap.

Who signed the PSA contract.

Who went out and found a mortgage for their commercial deal.

Who raised money with family and friends.

(And was probably scared every step of the way.)

If YOU are that woman, or know of a woman like this-

Pls let me know in the below comments.

#investing #cre #overcomingfear #warriors

83   71 Comments

Instagram Story Video with Poll Sticker:

Poll stickers are one of the best ways to increase engagement via Stories.

Barbara Betts, Broker & CEO The Betts Realty Group
@barbbetts

LinkedIn Single Image Post with Long Form Text Description:

LinkedIn Video Post with Text description:
Eddie Gonzalez, Retail Sales & Leasing SVN Desert Commercial Advisors

Facebook Status Update:

Phil Treadwell, VP Development Mason-McDuffie Mortgage
@philtreadwell

Facebook Story with Poll Sticker:

Instagram Carousel Post:

Neel Dhingra, Branch Manager All Western Mortgage

@neelhome

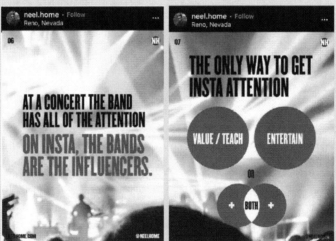

**This post is both shareable and bookmark worthy because its visual, swipeable(engaging) and educational!

LinkedIn Vertical Video with Captions:

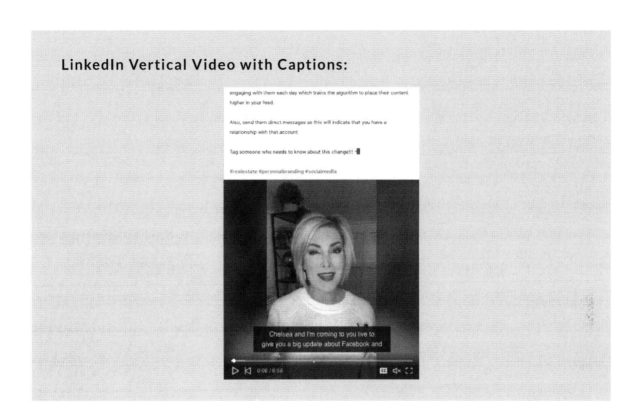

LinkedIn Image Post with Long Form Text:

Barry Wolfe shares an eye-catching infographic and poses question in text.

Barry Wolfe, Sr Managing Director Investments, Wolfe Retail Group, Marcus & Millichap

Linkedin.com/in/barrywolfecre

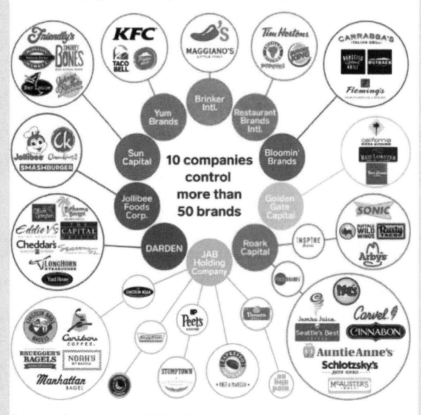

Barry Wolfe • 1st

#NetLeasePro | Commercial Real Estate | Single Tenant Net Lease | 1031 Exchanges | Sale-Leasebacks | Shopping C...
1mo

I posted the below image earlier this summer.

There's already been a few changes—most recently, the addition yesterday of Jimmy John's to the menu of holdings by Inspire Brands.

As the parent company of Inspire Brands, Roark Capital Group has become a behemoth in the restaurant industry and the entire retail sector.

I expect the consolidation of brands to continue. Companies like Roark and Inspire will continue to acquire brands and grow their profile.

Do you see this as a positive for the industry or do you have concerns?

#NetLeasePro #shoppingandtheretailindustry #commercialrealestate #retailtrends #retail

ENTERTAINING

Entertaining = Personality + Relatability

People are always attracted to personality and of course fun! Entertaining content can be as simple as sharing a meme or a humorous story from your day.

Don't be afraid to let your real personality shine through your content (video is the best format for this). It's not unprofessional to be yourself, it's authentic!

Examples

- Share a "caption this" post with a funny photo
- Share your best "dad" joke of the day
- What "National Day" is today Example: Donut Day
- Most embarrassing moment

Facebook Image Post:

This post featured hilarious Snapchat face filters. The best and most unexpected part of this content was from the community testing out the filter!

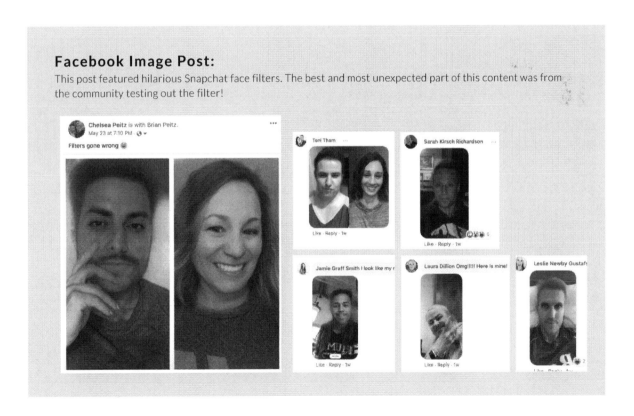

Snapchat Stories:

Sonia turns "boring" topics such as mold remediation, finger printing and closing escrow into fun micro videos.

Sonia Figueroa, Realtor eXp Realty

@soniafigueroare

YouTube Video:

Karin shares a funny parody video about the glamorous life of a realtor.

Karin Carr, Realtor http://bit.ly/karinyoutube

Facebook Business Page Image Post (originally a Snapchat Story):

Dustin Brohm, Realtor and creator of SearchSaltLake.com created his own 'meme' that was not only humorous but relatable to any Salt Lake locals

Facebook.com/searchsaltlake

YouTube Video & Facebook Single Image Post:

Shannon created a video parody of the popular Netflix series, Stranger Things, for her new listing and also promoted the video with a themed family photo on Facebook

Shannon Milligan, Realtor, RVA Home Team powered by eXp Realty
@rvahometeam

Instagram Story:

Black Haggett shares daily lip sync videos which built his brand and created engagement

Blake Hagett, Commerical Real Estate Advisor
KZB Real Estate @ Boise Premier Real Estate
@blake_hagzre

Instagram Story:

Sue "Pinky" Benson shares historical tips about her neighborhood in "Fun Fact Friday" series

Sue "Pinky" Benson, Realtor Re/Max Realty Team
@pinkyknowsnaples

Tik Tok Videos:

Tanner shows his personality and his listings with creative video clips

Tanner Richie, Realtor Compass
@tannerrichie

Facebook Business Page Video:

Movement mortgage marketing team creates hilarious movie parodies that showcase their humor and transform mundane content into pure entertainment

Jake Fehling, VP Marketing Movement Mortgage
@jakefehling

Twitter Post using GIF:

Gabriel Gonzalez, Commercial Landlord Rep Regency Centers
@gabriel_crenerd

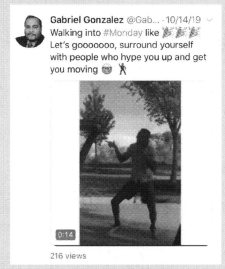

EXCLUSIVE

We all like to feel like insiders!

Often, we think exclusive means a grand reveal or announcement, however, it can also mean sharing behind the scenes of your business and your life.

Don't be afraid that your life is "too boring." There is "magic in the mundane," meaning that we connect through everyday commonalities.

Examples

- Top takeaways from a public event, training or conference
- Sneak peek of your free download or lead magnet
- Day in the life of an agent/lender
- Sharing your recent home remodel progress pics

Instagram Feed Post:

Backstage meet and greet with Gary Vee

Instagram Story:

Prepping for live webinar

Facebook Image Post:

Day in the life of a speaker

Instagram Single Image Feed Post:

Travis shares a sneak peek of his upcoming conference slides

Travis Thom, Owner Elevated Real Estate Marketing
@travis.thom

Instagram Story:

Sneak Peak of Katie's private mastermind retreat and content guide

Katie Lance, Real Estate Coach, Author, Speaker
Katielance.com

Facebook Multiple Image Post with Descriptive Text:

Nima gives an insider look into what happens on a TV station set with a mixture of still images and videos

Nima Khanghahi, Agent Growth Manager Opendoor

@nimathespeaker

LinkedIn Live Video Interview:

Live Video host Virgie Van Horst interviews me about the Science of Social Selling and a pre-release book sneak peek.

Virgie Van Horst, VH Realty Group

linkedin.com/in/virgievanhorst

Instagram Video Post With Captions:

Geoff hosts exclusive interview with industry insiders and provides a 1 minute sneak peek clip

Geoff Zimpfer, Natl Sales Coach Movement Mortgage and Host of Mortgage Marketing Radio Podcast
Mortgagemarketinginstitute.com

Instagram Giveaway Post:

Jason Cassity, Realtor® Compass
@jason_cassity

*Hosting a Giveaway via Instagram is an excellent way to grow your audience in a short amount of time AND generate high levels of engagement on a post!

Instagram Story Highlight Album:

I created an album dedicated to sneak peek Instagram Stories of the creation of this workbook!

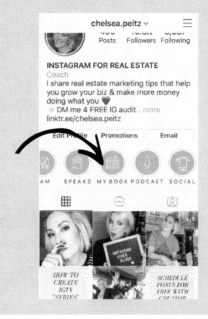

Online Training Modules:

Judi Fox, LinkedIn Expert &Coach

Linkedin.com/in/judiwfox

Judifox.com

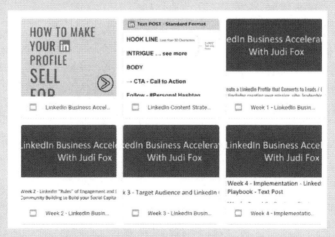

*Online training course, slide decks and webinars are excellent sources of inspiration for your social media posts – snippets and sneak peeks!

Private Facebook Group:

Elevated Real Estate Marketing Mastermind, Travis Thom

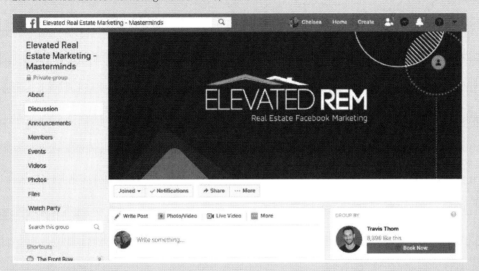

*Post exclusive content only available to this group, host Watch Parties and create learning "Units" within your Group that allow members to access libraries of content organized by topic.

EMOTIONAL

Humanize yourself through personal (not necessarily private) content.

Give your audience a reason to connect to you and see themselves in a shared story.

We connect with people when we feel that they are relatable in some way.

Our experiences can provide people with value. It doesn't have to be related to work at all - we may connect with someone based on their personal struggles or their business experiences.

Someone who entertains us, makes us laugh or brightens our day is providing value.

Examples

- Share your bucket list goals and ask viewers to share theirs

- Pose questions about specific scenarios and ask for input
  For example: "Today I received an interesting email and I wanted to know what your response would be" or "Have you ever felt....?"

- Nostalgia posts about your childhood or community then and now - ask people if they remember and to share their experiences!

Facebook Single Image Post:

This post focuses on NOSTALGIA which is a powerful emotional trigger!

So many comments sharing their own memories of this iconic burger joint!

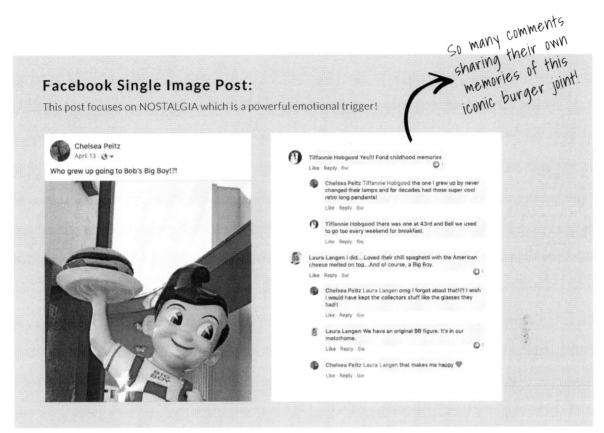

Facebook Status Update:

Text with color background focused on nostalgia

LinkedIn Text Post:

This post focused on RELATABILITY. Asking your audience if they can relate to an issue that you experienced creates a human connection.

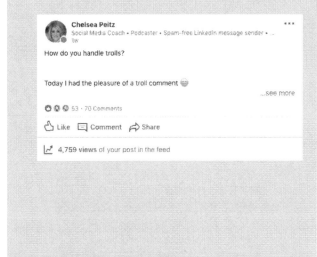
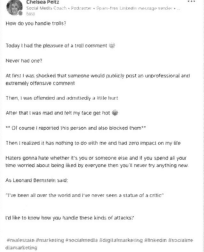

Instagram Single Image Feed Post with Text Overlay:

Positive or motivational quotes using personal photos

Arjun Dhingra, Licensed mortgage banker
@arjunmortgage

All Western Mortgage, Inc.

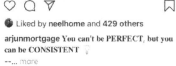

Instagram Single Image Feed Post:

Text overlay photo quotes

Gabriel Gonzalez, Commercial Landlord Rep Regency Centers
@gabriel_crenerd

Website Review:

Judi Fox, LinkedIn Expert & Coach
JudiFox.com

Beena Miller
I Help Service-Based Businesses Build A Brand On Social Media + Results•Follow Zaney Marketing
July 27, 2019, Beena was a client of Judi's

JUDI FOX ROCKS! 🦊 Judi is the REAL DEAL when it comes to LinkedIn coaching. I saw Judi being interviewed on a LinkedIn live with Dr. Ai (Classroom Without Walls) and immediately realized that this gal knows her stuff and is not afraid to share the secret-sauce to LinkedIn. I own a boutique social media agency and wanted to be able to bring real strategies to my LinkedIn clients and realized Judi is who I needed to learn from. Judi truly understands the nuances of LinkedIn platform and Judi coached me to truly transform how to market myself on this very unique platform with content and video. I would HANDS DOWN recommend Judi's LinkedIn Like A Fox coaching program as it has been invaluable for me and for my clients. Thank you so much Judi for all that you do and your awesomeness on this platform!!

*Reviews are excellent for building your brand credibility, SEO and also sharing screenshots to your social media platforms!

Facebook Album Post:

Haley Parker, Area Business Development Manager, Fairway Independent Mortgage
@haley_parker_

Facebook Live Series & Podcast Episodes:

Marki Lemons Rhyal, Real Estate Social Media Speaker & Author of The Modern Real Estate
Professionals Guide to Success
Markilemons.com

Facebook Live Series: Parenthood and Believing that You Can do Anything
Posted on September 17, 2019 by Marki Lemons · 9 Comments

While we've all had to deal with naysayers at some point in our lives, we also need to own up to the fact that sometimes, we might be our own naysayers – or worse – someone else's. Even though we may think we're 'keeping it 100' by being what we think is realistic about other.... Continue Reading

Filed Under: Podcast

Facebook Live Series 2: Why I Left Pharma Sales for Real Estate and Never Looked Back
Posted on September 10, 2019 by Marki Lemons · 0 Comments

Early in my career, I was balancing two careers, as a pharmaceutical rep and as a real estate agent. Even though it seemed impossible, I was the top earner in pharma sales, and then I successfully switched to real estate full-time, and made more in a month than I ever would in MONTHS of pharmaceutical.... Continue Reading

Refer to the following page for extra notes on the ins and outs of Emotional content

PERSONAL VS PRIVATE: A VERY IMPORTANT PIECE OF THE EMOTIONAL CONTENT EQUATION

Consumers want to see the real person behind the brand. Vulnerability creates trust and relatability which are the two most important elements of forming a solid relationship.

This doesn't mean that you need to burst into tears on a live broadcast or rant about your frustrations, but it could mean sharing with your audience that your car broke down, your coffee spilled on you or your youngest is headed off to college and how that makes you feel.

When we see others experience emotions, happiness, laughter or sadness, our own neurons fire in the same way. We see ourselves in those people's experiences and this is what connects us as a community. At the end of the day, we want to work with humans not algorithms.

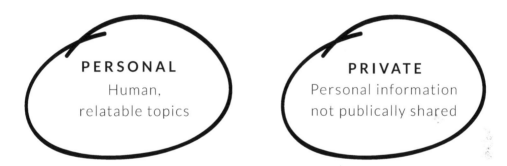

EXAMPLE OF HOW TO SHARE A PERSONAL CONTENT PIECE WITHOUT SHARING THE PRIVATE PORTION OF IT:

Think about the topic that you consider "private" and then ask yourself, "Is there a part of that idea that would be publicly shareable that others may enjoy or could spark conversation?"

Ultimately, YOU decide what you want to share with the world. My only advice is to stay safe and stay legal

- Imagine meeting a client for dinner. You may share a photo of the restaurant sign and ask your audience if they've ever dined there before and engage in conversation. What you DON'T post is the photos of your dinner companions or broadcast the conversations taking place at the table.

- You've just checked into a fabulous luxury resort. You might share a breathtaking photo of the sunset view but you may not share a tour of your suite.

- You share your day to day activities, however, you prefer to not show your children's faces in the photos or videos.

Fill in your own
5 E Content
ideas below

EDUCATIONAL

ENTERTAINING

ENGAGING

EMOTIONAL

EXCLUSIVE

CRAFT QUALITY CONTENT CONSISTENTLY

"Stop writing about everything. So many brands create content and try to cover everything, instead of focusing on the core niche that they can position themselves as an expert around. No one cares about your special recipe... Find your niche, and then go even more niche."

Joe Pulizzi, Author

261 DAYS OF CONTENT IDEAS

One idea for every **week day** of the year

———

100 real estate topics

EDUCATIONAL

1. SERIES: "Best Of" the neighborhood (top 5 coffee shops, pizza, gyms etc)

2. SERIES: "Battle Of" (restaurants, area, schools)

3. SERIES: "Meet the Experts" - interview or review local area experts (pediatricians, dentist, specialists)

4. SERIES: "How Much Does It Cost" (remodeling, movers, building a pool)

5. Best places for a staycation in your neighborhood

6. The benefits of working with an iBuyer and how an agent can help

7. Do you really need to hire a real estate agent?

8. Create a "How To" or "Explainer" video about the home buying/selling, mortgage and escrow processes

9. Should you short sell your home?

10. First time home buying mistakes

11. The biggest myths about home loans/down payments/iBuyers

12. What is wire fraud and common scams you need to know about

13. New home construction – do you need an agent?

14. What happens if you still haven't sold your home but have to relocate?

15. What is a contingency?

16. Yikes! You sold your house faster than you had planned, now what?

17. What to do if you receive multiple offers

18. What to expect during your corporate relocation process

19. What to expect during your Permanent Change of Station (PCS) [military relocation]

- [ ] **20.** Do you really need a home warranty?
- [ ] **21.** Do you need title insurance?
- [ ] **22.** New construction homes: is the price negotiable?
- [ ] **23.** How to buy a foreclosed home
- [ ] **24.** How to sell your own home for the best price without an agent
- [ ] **25.** Beware of these common real estate scams
- [ ] **26.** Neighborhood resource lists (utility companies, local schools etc)
- [ ] **27.** What is a due diligence period?
- [ ] **28.** Are open houses really worth it?
- [ ] **29.** Should you use a lockbox for your property?
- [ ] **30.** Do you need flood insurance?
- [ ] **31.** How to win a bidding war in a hot market
- [ ] **32.** How to find a qualified General Contractor/Interior Designer etc
- [ ] **33.** # questions to ask your potential Realtor at your first meeting
- [ ] **34.** Market Update for your area

- [ ] **35.** Top # mistakes you don't want to make with your rental property
- [ ] **36.** # steps every homebuyer must take before looking at properties
- [ ] **37.** SERIES: "Best thing on the menu" at local restaurants
- [ ] **38.** How to challenge a low appraisal
- [ ] **39.** How to clean the smell of smoke/ pet dander from a home
- [ ] **40.** Can you rent to own?
- [ ] **41.** When to turn on/off your utilities when moving
- [ ] **42.** Do you need an appraisal before listing?
- [ ] **43.** Can you take back your offer? (Can you get our of your contract)
- [ ] **44.** Should you write a letter to the seller?
- [ ] **45.** Renovation loans/VA Loans/FHA Loans – how do they work?
- [ ] **46.** SERIES: Best places to eat if you're health conscious or on a specific meal plan
- [ ] **47.** Best pet sitter/kennel in the neighborhood
- [ ] **48.** My Story: why I became a realtor/ mortgage/title professional

- [ ] **49.** Interview your team members or industry partners
- [ ] **50.** Design trends for the coming season/year
- [ ] **51.** Share info on FREE local events – farmers markets, holiday lights, pumpkin patches
- [ ] **52.** Solar panels – What you need to know
- [ ] **53.** What are liens and judgments and how do they affect your transaction?
- [ ] **54.** New home model home tours
- [ ] **55.** What is a transfer tax?
- [ ] **56.** Meet your local mayor/city employee/local official
- [ ] **57.** Best hotels/vacation rentals in your area for visiting family and friends
- [ ] **58.** The # biggest deal killers
- [ ] **59.** The # mistakes that sellers make
- [ ] **60.** Short term / vacation rentals, are they allowed?
- [ ] **61.** What do you need to know if you purchase a home and don't reside in the US?

- [ ] **62.** Do videos sell homes?
- [ ] **63.** Should you get professional staging for your listing?
- [ ] **64.** How much value does (new feature) add to your home?
- [ ] **65.** How to sell vacant land
- [ ] **66.** How to sell a home with a specific style/decor/location
- [ ] **67.** Should you do "coming soon" marketing?
- [ ] **68.** # reasons to list your home before the holidays/during the holidays
- [ ] **69.** How to show your home with kids/pets
- [ ] **70.** What is a "smart home"?
- [ ] **71.** How quickly can you close?
- [ ] **72.** Who pays for what?
- [ ] **73.** Pre-qualification vs pre-approval
- [ ] **74.** How to find the right mortgage/real estate/title professional
- [ ] **75.** Should you remodel or just drop the price?
- [ ] **76.** Zero down payment loan options

- [ ] **77.** How to save big with end of the year tax credits
- [ ] **78.** What happens down at the county recorders office?
- [ ] **79.** Buying a condo: what you need to know
- [ ] **80.** Why your house isn't selling?
- [ ] **81.** Does being self employed negatively impact your ability to get financing?
- [ ] **82.** FHA Loans and condos: what you need to know
- [ ] **83.** How is the luxury market different?
- [ ] **84.** Is the market shifting?
- [ ] **85.** Is Zillow's Zestimate accurate? Why or why not?
- [ ] **86.** Inherited property sales tips
- [ ] **87.** # questions to ask before moving into assisted living
- [ ] **88.** What *exactly* do you have to disclose as a seller?
- [ ] **89.** Moving soon? Don't forget these last minute tips!
- [ ] **90.** Rent back agreements: What Sellers/Buyers need to know
- [ ] **91.** What is pre-occupancy?
- [ ] **92.** Showing etiquette - what not to do
- [ ] **93.** What conveys in the sale of your property?
- [ ] **94.** Flipping houses: what you need to know
- [ ] **95.** How to evict a tenant
- [ ] **96.** How to repair your credit
- [ ] **97.** Can you get a special loan for a "fixer upper"?
- [ ] **98.** Can you buy a home after bankruptcy?
- [ ] **99.** (CITY NAME) Jobs: Top # Employers
- [ ] **100.** How to prepare your home for a natural disaster

BRAINSTORM 10 MORE LOCAL COMMUNITY TOPICS!

ENGAGING, EXCLUSIVE, ENTERTAINING, EMOTIONAL

- **101.** What is your Unique Value Proposition?

- **102.** What is one thing about your job that would surprise most people?

- **103.** Has this ever happened to you? (forgetting shoes, 4 flat tires, etc)

- **104.** Are you a technophobe?

- **105.** Did you have a Blackberry? Do you miss it?

- **106.** Have you ever felt like...

- **107.** Share a perceived failure and what you learned from it

- **108.** One thing that people would be surprised to learn about you

- **109.** The book you're reading now or one that's inspired you

- **110.** A podcast you're listening to – ask for recommendations

- **111.** Bloopers and outtakes videos

- **112.** Most embarrassing moment

- **113.** What apps are on your home screen?

- **114.** Best apps for meditation/ productivity/photo editing

- **115.** The purchase under $100 that has most impacted your life

- **116.** Poll: Ask your audience for advice or recommendation ex: "What Netflix show should I watch next?"

- **117.** Your hidden talent or superpower?

- **118.** Thank someone who has been a mentor in your life

- **119.** Share your morning/night routine

- **120.** Biggest obstacle or challenge you've overcome

- **121.** Do you play an instrument – can you show an example in a video?

- **122.** Do you meal plan? Keto? Gluten Free? Tips or Recipes you can share?

- **123.** Unboxings!

- **124.** Life Hacks – tips for parents or pet owners?

- **125.** What's on your bucket list?

- **126.** Do you have a recurring dream?

- **127.** Favorite family fun night location or date nite idea

- **128.** Social media, phone or email scams warning

- [ ] **129.** What's the weirdest thing in your purse? Trunk? Gym Bag? Glove box?
- [ ] **130.** The best thing to do everyday to become a better (spouse, parent, employee etc)
- [ ] **131.** What's your best tip to get "unstuck"
- [ ] **132.** These # books will change your life
- [ ] **133.** What sticky note do you have on your mirror/computer?
- [ ] **134.** Guilty Pleasures – do you watch reality tv shows? Eat in bed?
- [ ] **135.** Best tip for getting your kids to do chores/read
- [ ] **136.** How many states have you lived in?
- [ ] **137.** What are your favorite conferences to attend?
- [ ] **138.** Top takeaways from a recent event
- [ ] **139.** What's your #1 goal for the year?
- [ ] **140.** What's the last movie you saw in the movie theater?
- [ ] **141.** What makes your mom/sister/ brother/dad better than others (tag them!)
- [ ] **142.** If you could replay one moment from your life what would it be and why?
- [ ] **143.** What's your go-to, easy-to-make quick dinner recipe?
- [ ] **144.** What song describes you/your spouse to a tee?
- [ ] **145.** Confession: I collect/I'm afraid of/ I haven't …
- [ ] **146.** What's the best wifi name you've seen
- [ ] **147.** Looking for the best _____ restaurant in ___ - GO!
- [ ] **148.** Do you still read the newspaper?
- [ ] **149.** I'm afraid to ask, but iPhone or Droid?
- [ ] **150.** Best epic movie of all time?
- [ ] **151.** Share a weird habit & ask if others do it too (ex:talking to yourself)
- [ ] **152.** Do you wake up with a song in your head?
- [ ] **153.** What would you say to your 20 year old self?
- [ ] **154.** "Caption this" (Use this call to action along with a funny or interesting photo post)
- [ ] **155.** Trivia posts
- [ ] **156.** Funny memes
- [ ] **157.** Positive Quotes

- [ ] **158.** One food you cannot live without?
- [ ] **159.** What was the last thing you got really excited about?
- [ ] **160.** What's the one movie you can watch over and over?
- [ ] **161.** If you could only have one app on your phone what would it be?
- [ ] **162.** What are you thankful for today?
- [ ] **163.** At what age do you think kids should learn to (cook/get a phone)
- [ ] **164.** Work with a charity - Talk about it!
- [ ] **165.** "Foster Friday" – feature adoptable pets from local shelters
- [ ] **166.** Share the istory of different neighborhood landmarks or locations
- [ ] **167.** Time to get deeeeep... what does [.........] mean to you?
- [ ] **168.** What's the next car you're going to buy?
- [ ] **169.** Share someone else's content and tag them (Always include your opinion or original content describing why you are sharing!)
- [ ] **170.** What's happening in your industry?
- [ ] **171.** Product reviews
- [ ] **172.** What are your most used emojis?
- [ ] **173.** What emoji do you wish they had in your keyboard?
- [ ] **174.** Host a giveaway or contest
- [ ] **175.** Favorite Disney character?
- [ ] **176.** Team cat or team dog?
- [ ] **177.** Coffee or tea?
- [ ] **178.** Netflix in pjs or late night on the town?
- [ ] **179.** Facebook or Instagram?
- [ ] **180.** Mountains or Beach?
- [ ] **181.** Margaritas – frozen or on the rocks?
- [ ] **182.** Pepsi or Coke?
- [ ] **183.** If you could retire tomorrow what would you spend the rest of your life doing?
- [ ] **184.** If you could only eat one thing for the rest of your life, what would it be?
- [ ] **185.** What is the 1 thing you can't live without (can't be family or phone!)
- [ ] **186.** What's the best thing to do in your hometown?
- [ ] **187.** How many houses have you lived in?
- [ ] **188.** TV has become nothing but ___

- [ ] **189.** I wish they made ____ like they used to
- [ ] **190.** You went to the University of _____
- [ ] **191.** Your favorite blog is ____
- [ ] **192.** Your all time favorite book is _____
- [ ] **193.** You're going to _____ today if it kills you!
- [ ] **194.** Your Monday/Sunday morning must have is _____
- [ ] **195.** Share a boomerang or time lapse video
- [ ] **196.** Share your favorite "dad" or "mom" joke
- [ ] **197.** National "Day" posts ex: National Donut Day
- [ ] **198.** Interview your parent, child or spouse
- [ ] **199.** Ask others what 3 words describe you
- [ ] **200.** Do you believe in ghosts?
- [ ] **201.** Ever lived in a haunted house?
- [ ] **202.** Do you regret your tattoo
- [ ] **203.** Go-to cold/flu remedies
- [ ] **204.** Best resources to keep you motivated
- [ ] **205.** Favorite meditation or mental health tips
- [ ] **206.** "Ask Me Anything" post
- [ ] **207.** Insider tips to (Disney/cruising/Europe)
- [ ] **208.** Favorite place to shop for _____
- [ ] **209.** Best activities in your area for kids by age group
- [ ] **210.** One bad habit you want to break this year
- [ ] **211.** Do you vision board/journal?
- [ ] **212.** What lesson did you learn this week?
- [ ] **213.** Where is the strangest place you've ever fallen asleep?
- [ ] **214.** 2 truths and a lie (post 2 true things and 1 lie and see who can guess correctly!)
- [ ] **215.** What's the one word you constantly misspell?
- [ ] **216.** How to get over the fear of _____
- [ ] **217.** Favorite coffee mug (or other common item)
- [ ] **218.** What's the most unusual thing you eat for breakfast?
- [ ] **219.** How long is your commute?
- [ ] **220.** What's on your Audible/nightstand?
- [ ] **221.** TV: on or off at dinner?

222. Are social media platforms violating your privacy?

223. Is social media making the world better?

224. Your biggest pet peeve is _____

225. The last thing you bought was_____

226. Do you still have a land line?

227. Do you still have a printer or are you all digital?

228. How do you get your news?

229. What was the most unique college course you've ever taken?

230. How many countries have you been to and which was your favorite?

231. It's hard to get up and work out in cold weather, any ideas for motivation?

232. Back to school: Best advice for kindergarten/jr high/high school freshmen

235. Time to take a trip: best carry on packing tips

236. Which musician's death has had the biggest impact on the music industry?

237. What's the strangest thing in your room (you're not allowed to explain why it's there!)

238. What was your favorite childhood toy (can you find a photo of it?)

239. Where was your favorite place to hang out as a kid/teen?

240. What was the first car you remember your parents driving?

241. What was your first car?

242. What was your first concert?

243. Share a throwback photo of prom

244. Did you eat at a popular restaurant that is no longer around? What did you order?

245. "Remember this?" post (share photo of old landmark that isn't there or old tech)

246. Video or board games from your childhood

247. What did you want to be when you grew up?

248. Best song of the (70s, 80s, 90s)

249. Did you play sports as a kid?

250. The worst haircut or outfit you had as a kid (bonus if you can find photo!)

251. Where were you when "x" happened?

252. The best advice your parents ever gave you

253. What's the one thing you hated eating as a kid but you love to eat now?

254. How far do you live from the place where you were born?

255. Which item from your childhood do you wish your parents had saved for you?

256. What was your first job? How old were you?

257. What was your high school mascot?

258. Which character in Breakfast Club (or another movie) describes you in high school?

259. Do you still talk to your high school best friend/boyfriend/girlfriend?

260. Who was your favorite teacher in high school and why?

261. Did you marry your high school sweetheart? How old were you when you got married?

TAKE ACTION

- Select 5 Content Starts (one for each "E" category)
- Post to the social of your choice (Facebook, IGTV, LinkedIn) one per week for 5 weeks or two per week for 3 weeks

BONUS CHALLENGE:
Create a short, 1 minute vertical video live or recorded as your post format!

CONQUER YOUR CONTENT FEARS

"The only thing you absolutely need to know is the location of the library."

Albert Einstein

Even more!

WHERE TO FIND CONTENT IDEAS

Top Websites, Apps and Tools for Your Content

Already used all 261 ideas? No problem! You can source endless inspiration for content ideas using these (mostly) free online tools:

CONTENT INSPIRATION RESOURCES

1. Google's "People Also Ask" section

This section of Google's search results provides endless topics related to your original search terms. Enter a keyword phrase into Google's search bar and scroll down the results page until you locate the "People also ask" results box.

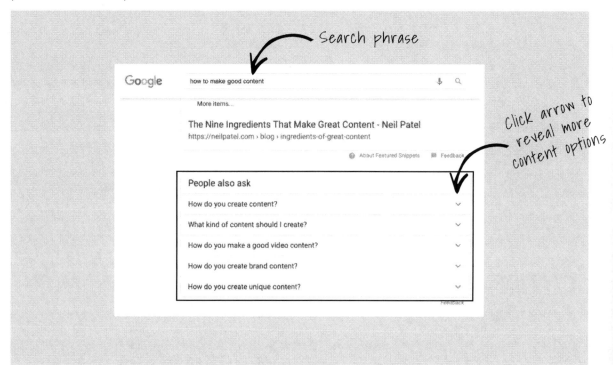

2. Set up Google Alerts for specific keywords, phrases or names

Google will send you emails when new results for a topic that you've followed show up in google search. Set up Alerts for your name, brand or company name and any other topics of interest!

www.google.com/alerts

3. Use Answerthepublic.com

A visual keyword tool that creates an image of related topics based on our search keywords.

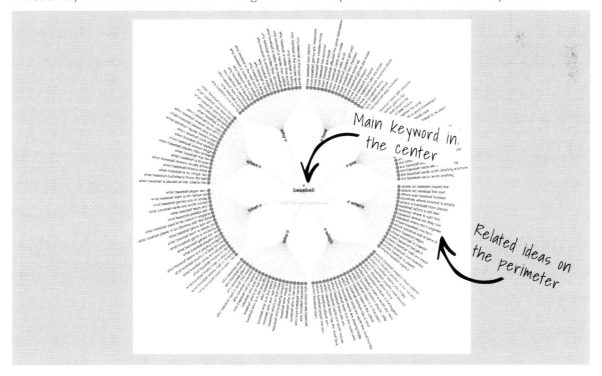

4. Feedly.com (also Feedly app)

A free news and blog aggregator that allows you to follow, organize and save content by topic.

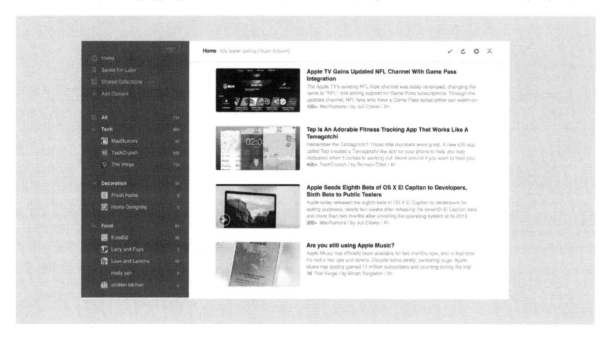

5. Buzzsumo.com

An online research and monitoring tool that organizes content ranked by social media shares. (Paid service starting at $99/mo)

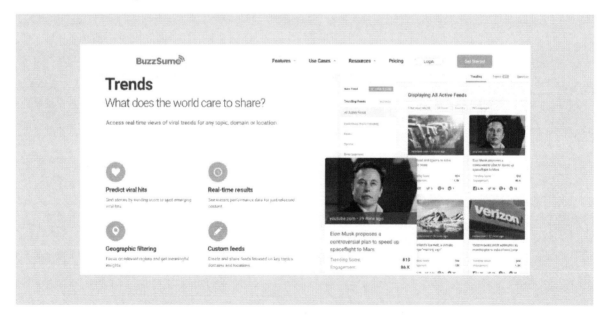

6. Ubersuggest.com

A website that helps you generate keyword ideas for your content marketing strategy.

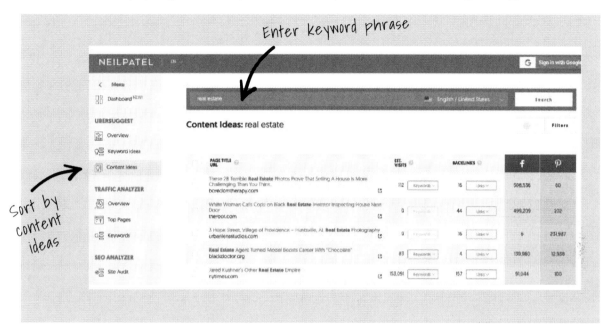

7. Facebook Groups

By using the search bar within any Facebook Group, you can search for keywords to help locate content ideas within a specific genre. Additionally, by listening to the Group posts, you can identify commonly asked questions that can inspire future content.

8. Keywords Everywhere Chrome Plugin

A browser add-on for Chrome & Firefox that shows search volume, CPC & competition on multiple websites.

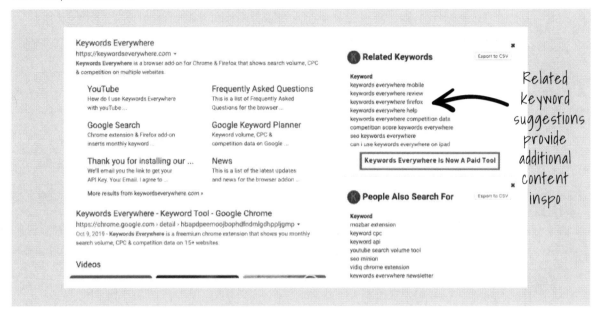

Related keyword suggestions provide additional content inspo

9. Scoop.it

Curated content sorted by topic, keyword or format.

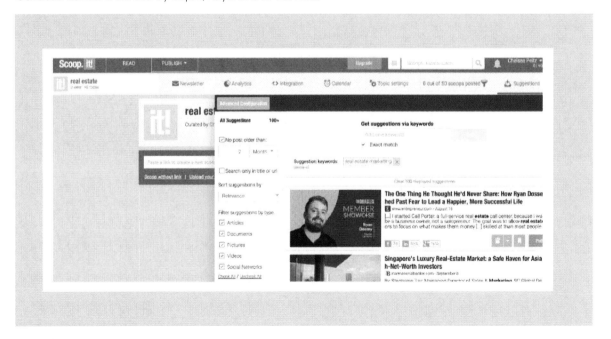

10. Reddit.com

A network of communities with crowdsourced content and discussions.

Search keyword phrase

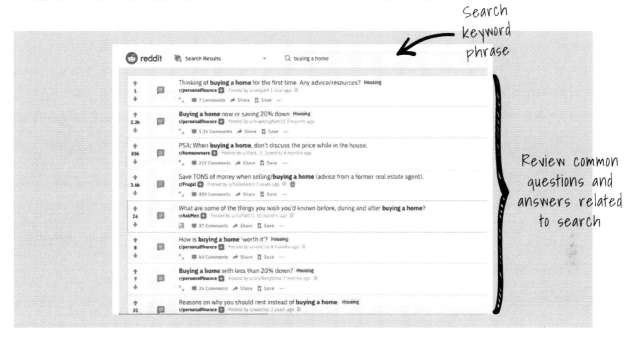

Review common questions and answers related to search

11. Quora.com

A question-and-answer website where questions are asked, answered, and edited by Internet users, either factually, or in the form of opinions.

Search keyword phrase

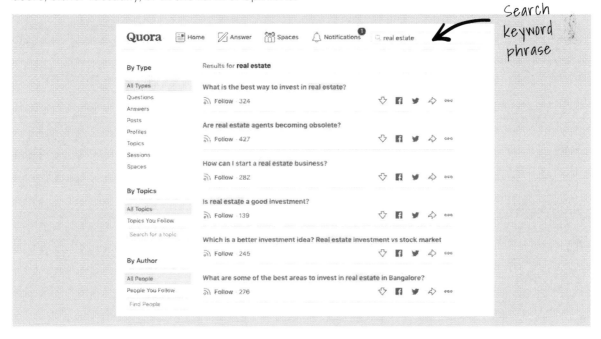

12. LinkedIn "Content" Search

A social media and content platform that also allows any user to perform searches by keyword and sort by "content" to view user posts related to that topic.

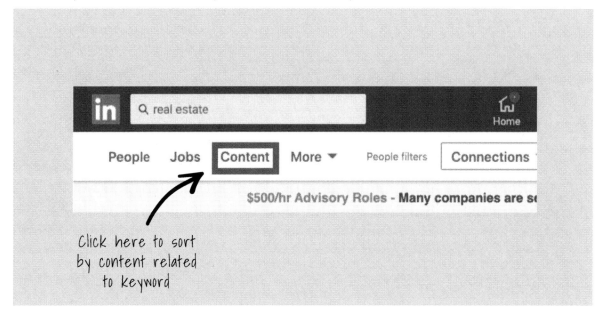

Click here to sort by content related to keyword

13. Medium.com

A crowd sourced blogging platform that allows anyone to create and publish blog articles on any topic.

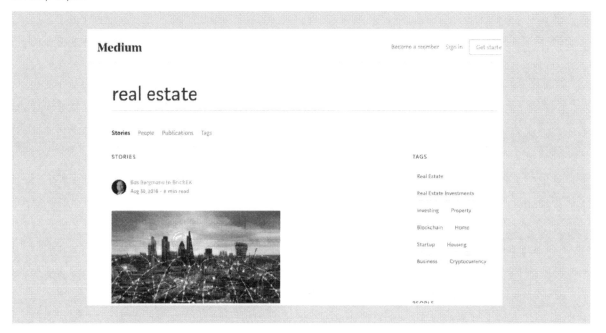

14. Pinterest

A social media network that allows users to share images and to visually discover new interests by browsing images others have posted. Think of it like a visual Google with the ability to save and organize content into "boards" and follow other users.

An easy way to use Pinterest to source content: Search a keyword and then sort by "Boards"

15. Twitter "Advanced Search"

A micro-blogging and social media site where users communicate through short text or visual posts.

To access "Advanced Search," enter a keyword into the search bar, then click on the blue "advanced search" phrase on the right hand side of the webpage.

Enter in terms in the below pop up window.

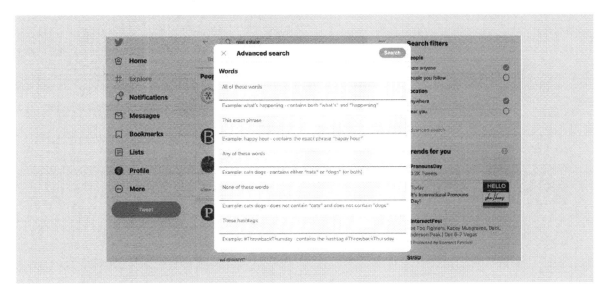

16. Podcast Episode Lists

Episode lists are a treasure trove of content inspiration for topics and guests. Check out your favorite podcasts' lists of episodes!

17. Books: Table of Contents

The old school podcast episode list... ☺

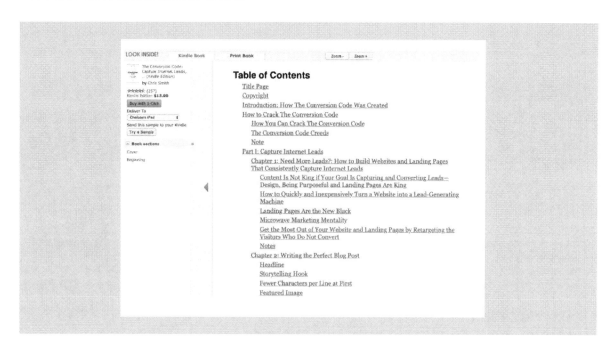

18. VidIQ Plugin (another alternative TubeBuddy)

A paid Chrome extension that provides information about keywords and suggests related keyword phrases (AKA, more content ideas) based on YouTube videos and search behavior.

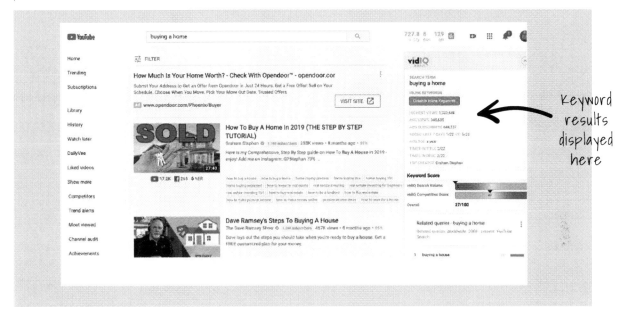

Keyword results displayed here

PRO TIP

Keep an idea file to ensure you never forget an idea in the moment! Use the notes app on your phone! If you want to get really techie, sign up for a free Trello account and organize your ideas digitally.

Now that you're oozing with content ideas, it's time to show you how to make the most of one piece of content or idea by using the "3 T Method" and Content Repurposing

Keep reading

THE "3 T" METHOD

A fail-proof method for creating content on a consistent basis without ever running out of ideas

---

Creating original content can feel a bit intimidating, even with examples and templates!

Some of the best content created has been inspired by some*one* or some*thing* else in our environment. Rest assured that virtually all content creators have been inspired by someone else's original idea or work.

This doesn't mean it's okay to plagiarize, steal, rip-off or even share someone else's content without giving them credit! Simply stated, content is all around you and has been created by someone at some point, all you have to do is consume it and become inspired!

Think about the content you already consume throughout the day: *Television, newspaper or newsblog, social media, movies, podcasts etc.*

There is at least one topic, tidbit or golden nugget you can glean from the content you're already engaging with on a regular basis.

Sharing an interesting fact, a helpful tip or your opinion is the easiest way to create your own original work.

For example, a non-fiction business book can provide you with helpful tips and when you implement them, you have fresh experiences and results that you can then turn into content.

Now you can enjoy the peace of mind that you will never run out of ideas or be required to create the original idea.

Let's get started!

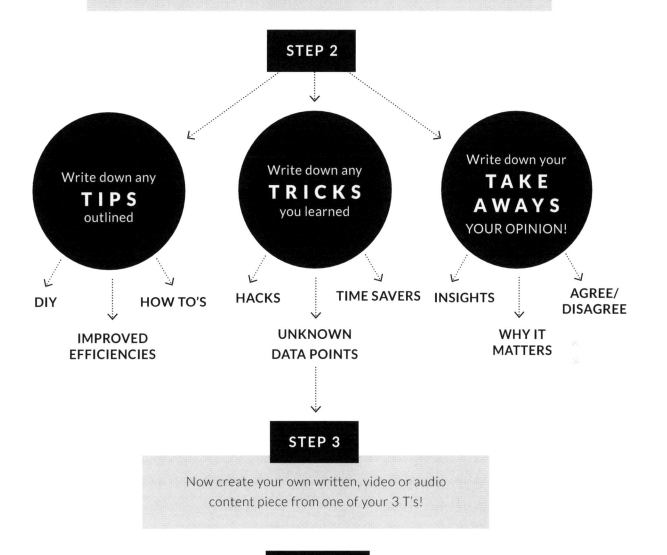

STEP 1

Find an article, podcast, blog post, news item, video or article. Read, watch or listen to it and then apply one (or more) of the following 3 T's

STEP 2

Write down any **TIPS** outlined

Write down any **TRICKS** you learned

Write down your **TAKE AWAYS** YOUR OPINION!

DIY

HOW TO'S

IMPROVED EFFICIENCIES

HACKS

TIME SAVERS

UNKNOWN DATA POINTS

INSIGHTS

AGREE/ DISAGREE

WHY IT MATTERS

STEP 3

Now create your own written, video or audio content piece from one of your 3 T's!

PRO TIP

Always credit the original source of the content piece you are referencing in your own content, provide a link if needed and @tag the author.

EXAMPLE OF THE "3 T" METHOD

To show you how to utilize the 3T Method we are going to use this article as an example...

3 Productivity Experts Explain Why Doing Less Actually Accomplishes More

Brianna Wiest Senior Contributor @ ForbesWomen

STEP 1
Find inspo content source, read take notes

STEP 2
Apply the "3 T" method

T1. Focus on a specific number of activities per day (Referenced "The One Thing" book)

T2. Why multi-tasking doesn't work (ask people if they multi-task)

T3. Not about doing more; it's about focusing less (give an example of this)

STEP 3
Create your own content. Tag/Link

Lastly, apply the "Deep Dive" Content Process to create additional topic starters from the above article:

Deep Dive this way

Once you've gone through the 3T process, create even more content ideas by taking a "Deep Dive" into your topic. Write down your main idea in the center of the page and brainstorm related topics.

EXAMPLE OF "DEEP DIVE" IDEA LIST

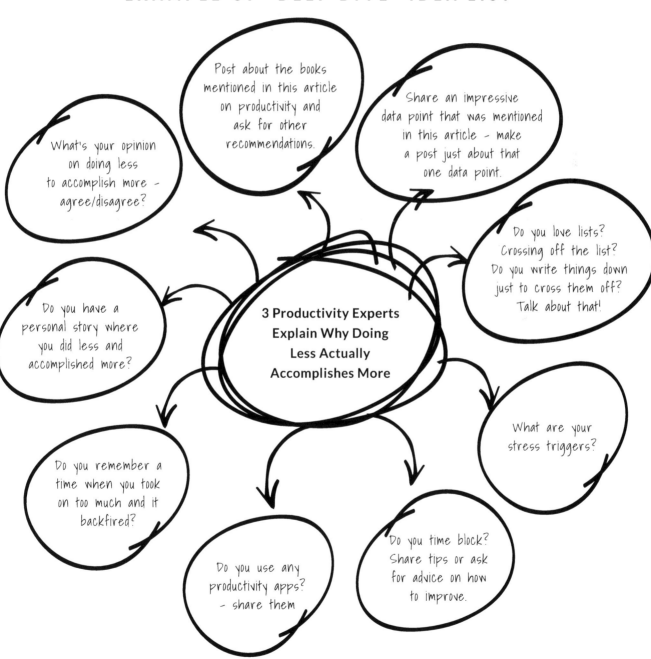

Your turn

ORIGINAL SOURCE CONTENT

YOUR T'S

DEEP DIVE IDEAS:

REPURPOSING CONTENT

Repurposing content allows you to create more content WITHOUT having to start over from scratch. Basically, it's a smart way to recycle a piece of content or re-use the same idea in a different format.

This strategy will help you reduce the pressure to produce new content and help you stay consistent.

Repurposing is NOT cross-posting, or posting the same *exact* piece of content to different platforms at the same time - either manually or through a scheduler or linked accounts.

There's nothing inherently wrong with cross-posting, however, many of us are active on multiple platforms and could see repeat content. Additionally, the formatting may not be optimized for a variety of platforms when cross-posted.

Here's an example of how to repurpose a Facebook Live video into additional pieces of content:

Edit original video and post 60 second clips with captions to Instagram and LinkedIn

Take a photo of you prepping for the Live video and post a behind the scenes content to your Stories (if you have swipe up capabilities, add a link)

Transcribe the live video into a blog post or extract quotable content and post as social media images with text overlay

Take a screenshot of your comments from the live video and post as content

Make a Facebook video ad using a portion of the live video optimized for video views

Create a slide deck of the top 5 takeaways from the live video

Make an infographic of the top takeaways

Create a YouTube Playlist or IGTV Series using your previous Facebook Lives on one topic

Post Instagram Feed Post Image of you recording the live video with a long form caption covering the topic of video

Try it out

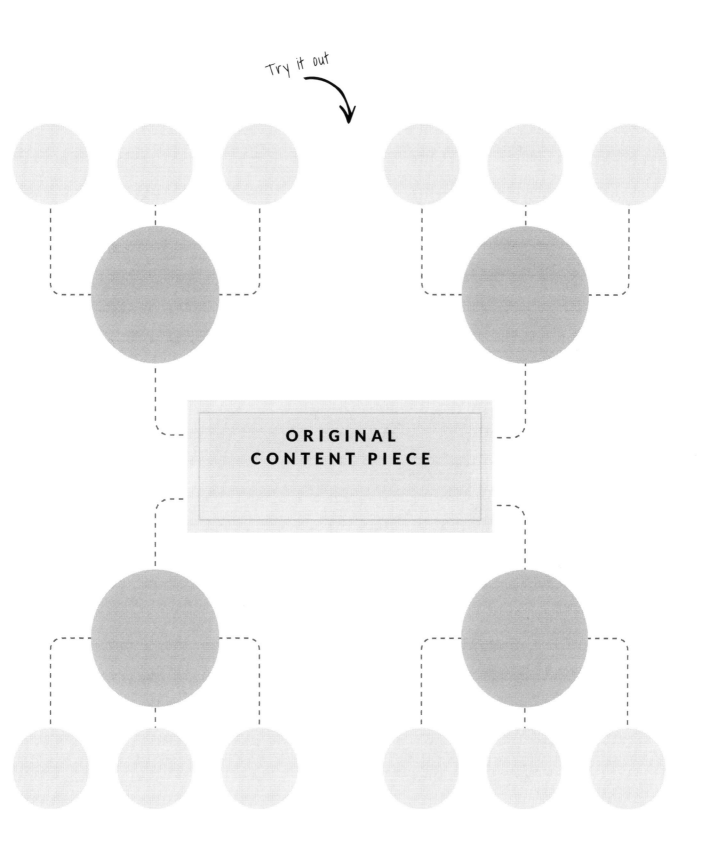

**ORIGINAL
CONTENT PIECE**

CONTENT FORMATS

You can repurpose your original content idea into dozens of different formats! One idea can inspire multiple future posts in a variety of formats:

A

Alexa Skill/Flash Briefing
Article for industry publication
Audio book

B

Blog Post
Book
Branded Items
Brochures

C

Case Studies
Charts
Chatbot script
Checklists
Collaborations
Contests

D

Digital Courses

I

In Person Events
Infographics
Interviews

R

Resource Lists
Reviews

E

eBook
Email Blast

L

Landing Page
Live Streams

S

Screenshots
Social Media posts
Surveys

F

FAQs
Flyers

M

Magazine
Memes
Mindmap

T

Templates
Templates
Testimonials
Text Blast

G

GIFS
Glossaries

N

Newsletter

V

Virtual trainings
Vlog

H

Hacks

Q

Q&As
Quote Images

W

Webinar
Website
White Papers

COPYWRITING THAT CONVERTS

"Writing isn't about using big words to impress. It's about using simple words in an impressive way."

Sierra Bailey, Author

HOW TO WRITE SOCIAL MEDIA CAPTIONS THAT GET MORE ENGAGEMENT

Once you've identified your content topics, it's equally as important (if not more) to write a compelling caption that generates engagement and inspires action. Captions provide context to your visual content and allow your posts to tell a deeper story that showcases your brand's voice and value.

 More importantly, a well-crafted caption can increase engagement, build community, drive web traffic, generate direct messages and ultimately, result in more leads.

Not only can captions create more conversions, but they also can boost your content's overall reach. The Socials track users' time spent engaging with content (reading/viewing), actions such as clicking on the (...see more) to open the entire caption and their overall reactions and comments to posts. The longer a user engages with your content, the better.

This chapter is made up of three sections to help you write better:

SECTION ONE: How to Write Headlines

SECTION TWO: Proven Copywriting Formulas

SECTION THREE: The Best Calls to Action

WHEN CREATING YOUR POST,
ASK YOURSELF THE FOLLOWING QUESTIONS

Who is this story for?
Why should they care?
What do they have to do next?

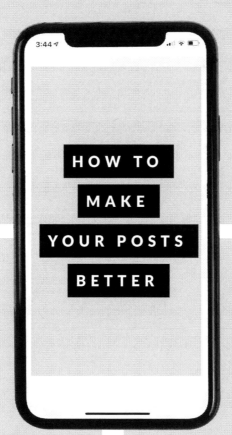

HOW TO
MAKE
YOUR POSTS
BETTER

CAPTURE ATTENTION

Capture attention with a compelling headline in the first sentence and then engage your audience with a call to action or question.

TELL A STORY

Tell a story that connects with your audience by crafting content from a perspective that will appeal to their needs and what matters to THEM! Remove the word "I" as much as possible from your captions.

THE ANATOMY OF A GOOD CAPTION

1. Headline/Hook:
An opening statement that grabs attention and hooks someone in to read further. Your goal should be to stop the scroll and entice the reader to read and take action.

2. Body:
The body of your caption describes your content (the image or video) and gives it context. It's the main story, lesson, or conversation. It's where you show your brand personality and communicate the meaning of your images and message.

3. Call to action:
A statement or question designed to get the reader to engage or take action - a direct command or a question.

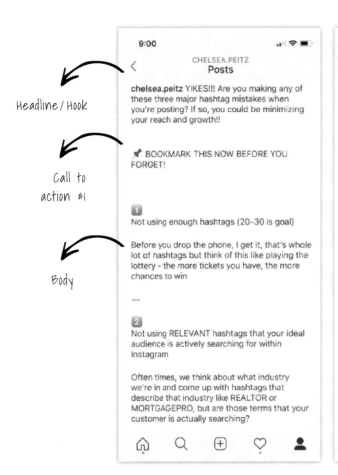

Headline / Hook

Call to action #1

Body

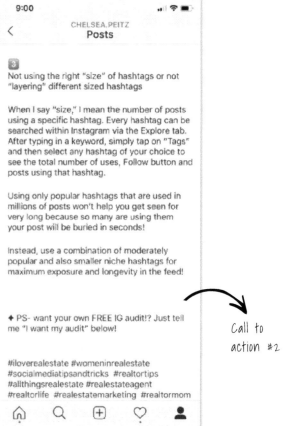

Call to action #2

1

CREATE ATTENTION GRABBING HEADLINES

YOUR HEADLINE IS THE FIRST, AND PERHAPS ONLY, IMPRESSION YOU MAKE ON A PROSPECTIVE READER.

Without a compelling promise that turns a browser into a reader, the rest of your words may as well not even exist. So, from a copywriting and content marketing standpoint, writing great headlines is a critical skill. 80% of readers never make it past the headline.

- Copyblogger

According to some sources, on average, eight out of 10 people will read headline copy, but only two out of 10 will read the rest.

Your first sentence or headline has two goals:

1.

Grab attention

2.

Entice people to read the next sentence

Writing headlines doesn't have to be intimidating! Luckily, there's tons of examples and templates used by professional copywriters that you can use as a guideline.

Let's get to it!

Buzzsumo.com, a content research tool, analyzed over 100 million headlines on Facebook and Twitter and reported on the following data points:

- Headline phrases that drive most engagement on Facebook

- Worst performing headline phrases on Facebook

- Most effective phrases that start or end headlines

- Optimum number of words and characters to use in a headline

- Most impactful numbers to use in headlines

- Most engaging Twitter headline phrases

- Differences between B2C and B2B headlines

The full report can be found here:
https://buzzsumo.com/blog/most-shared-headlines-study/

Below is a summary of their findings:

- Headlines with numbers received the highest levels of engagement

- The most powerful three word headline was "Will make you ..."
  Example: **5 Home Buying Tips That Will Make You Feel Smart**

- Emotional phrases received more engagement
  Example: **Shocked to see, Melt your heart, Can't stop laughing**

- Headline phrases that provoke curiosity gained a higher level of engagement
  Example: **What happened next, are freaking out, this is why, the reason is**

- Posts with twelve to eighteen words in the headline received the highest number of Facebook engagements

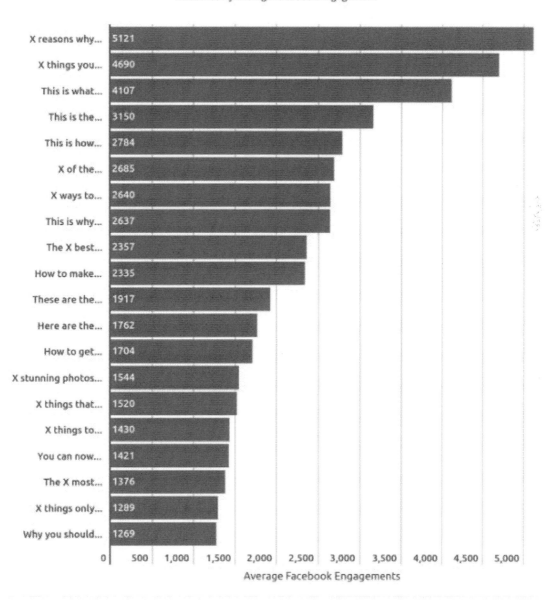

Top Phrases Starting Headlines

Measured by average Facebook Engagement

Phrase	Average Facebook Engagements
X reasons why…	5121
X things you…	4690
This is what…	4107
This is the…	3150
This is how…	2784
X of the…	2685
X ways to…	2640
This is why…	2637
The X best…	2357
How to make…	2335
These are the…	1917
Here are the…	1762
How to get…	1704
X stunning photos…	1544
X things that…	1520
X things to…	1430
You can now…	1421
The X most…	1376
X things only…	1289
Why you should…	1269

Average Facebook Engagements

2017 Review of 100m Articles
buzzsumo.com/blog/most-shared-headlines-study

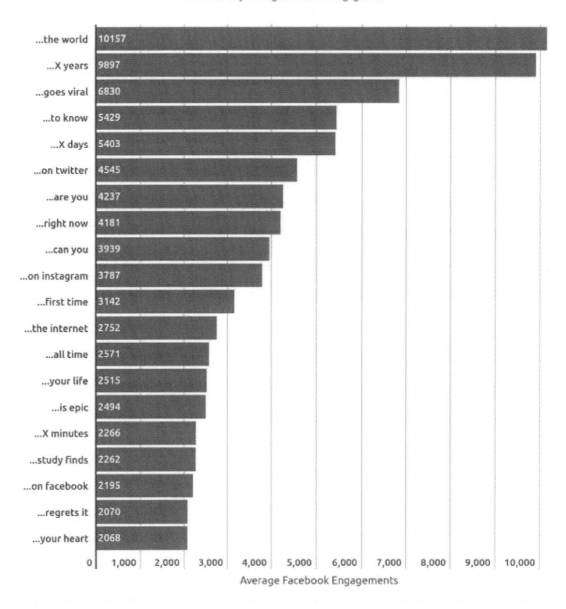

Top Phrases Ending Headlines
Measured by average Facebook Engagement

Phrase	Value
...the world	10157
...X years	9897
...goes viral	6830
...to know	5429
...X days	5403
...on twitter	4545
...are you	4237
...right now	4181
...can you	3939
...on instagram	3787
...first time	3142
...the internet	2752
...all time	2571
...your life	2515
...is epic	2494
...X minutes	2266
...study finds	2262
...on facebook	2195
...regrets it	2070
...your heart	2068

Average Facebook Engagements

2017 Review of 100m Articles
buzzsumo.com/blog/most-shared-headlines-study

HEADLINES THAT WILL HOOK YOUR READER

A Hook is defined as catchy sentence or paragraph in the introduction which serves as an attention-grabbing element. The effectiveness of the hook is defined by its ability to motivate people to read the entire text.

HOOK 'EM HEADLINE STARTERS

QUESTION

Pose a question that can be answered by your content or that peaks the reader's interest, motivates them to continue reading and/or invites the reader to engage.

Example: Have you ever considered selling your home without the help of a real estate agent?

STATISTIC

Share an interesting and relevant data point, fact or statistic from a credible source. Ideally, this stat should be impactful enough to elicit a response.

Example: 80% of new real estate agents have lost a client due to lack of online reviews

QUOTE

Use a quote from a well-known industry expert that supports your message.

Example: "Buying real estate is not only the best way, the quickest way, the safest way, but the only way to become wealthy" - Marshall Field

ADVICE

Become a trusted resource and build credibility through sharing personal expertise, anecdotes, tactics, insights, actionable tips, hacks, and how to's that your audience can put into practice.

Example: Remember you'll always regret what you didn't do rather than what you did.

DEFINITION

Educate your audience by defining a term or concept that is relevant to your area of expertise.

Example: An "iBuyer"; is the catchall term for online real estate investors who seek to reduce transactional property costs via digital tools. This kind of investor, for example, may use automated valuation models, instead of a bona fide appraiser, to make instant offers on homes to clients. They will also seek to minimize the involvement of real estate agents, often in favor of their own online listing services. The "i" in iBuyer, therefore, stands for "instant"; although many mistake it to mean "internet. - Housingwire.com

ANECDOTE/STORY

A personal story intended to persuade, inspire, caution or reminisce. The personal nature creates relatability between the storyteller and the reader.

Example: I remember when we closed on our first house! We had no idea what we were getting into at the beginning. Luckily, we found a Realtor who specialized in first time home buyers and she had a unique system that laid out everything we needed to do and by when step-by-step.

HUMOR

Entertain your audience with relatable and respectful humor.

Example: A real estate agent has 4 listings. Now add 5 more. What does the agent have now? Happiness. The agent has happiness.

DILEMMA

Present a scenario in which a choice must be made between two or more typically less than ideal options.

Example: The contractor said they could replace the roof and repair all of the water damage for $50,000 or could just remediate for 15K.

UNEXPECTED CLAIM

Highlight a surprising or potentially controversial statement that will entice your audience to read further.

Example: Realtors are the least trusted sales professional in 2019.

DESCRIPTION

Set the tone for your content with a descriptive intro that intrigues the reader.

Example: Shannon didn't know what to do. She panicked when she heard her client on the other end of the phone. They had just discovered that the roof of their brand new home had just caved in.

METAPHOR

Compare two seemingly unrelated topics and identify a relationship between them.

Example: Selling real estate is like running a marathon when it's 95 degrees in the dead of summer.

MAKE YOUR HEADLINES BETTER WITH POWER WORDS

Headlines that include emotional or power words receive more engagement and are shared more often. The Advanced Marketing Institute offers a free headline analyzer tool that assigns an Emotional Marketing Value (EMV). This number is a score that indicates how likely a headline is to elicit an emotional response from a reader.

Most professional copywriters' headlines will have 30%-40% EMV Words in their headlines, while the most gifted copywriters will have 50%-75% EMV words in headlines. A perfect score would be 100%, but that is rare unless your headline is less than five words.
- The Advanced Marketing Institute

WWW.AMINSTITUTE.COM/HEADLINE

Visit this website and type in any headline. Your headline will be analyzed and scored based on the total number of EMV words it has in relation to the total number of words it contains. This will determine the EMV score of your headline.

In addition to the EMV score, you will find out which emotion your headline most impacts.

Intellectual	Empathetic	Spiritual
Words which are especially effective when offering products and services that require reasoning or careful evaluation.	Words which resonate in with Empathetic impact often bring out profound and strong positive emotional reactions in people.	Words which havethe strongest potential for influence and often appeal to people at a very deep emotional level.

POWER WORDS FOR WRITING EMOTIONAL HEADLINES

Valuable	Sensational	Quick	Exclusive
Competitive	Confidential	Expert	Practical
Ultimate	Insider	Free	Unparalleled
Useful	Simplified	Urgent	Download
Innovative	Easy	Important	Special Offer
Excellent	Simple		

Additional resources:

https://sumo.com/stories/power-words
https://media.coschedule.com/uploads/write-emotional-headlines-power-words-copy.pdf

TOP 12 MOST INFLUENTIAL COPYWRITING WORDS

YOU	NEW	HEALTH	DISCOVER
MONEY	RESULTS	SAFETY	PROVEN
SAVE	GUARANTEED	LOVE	EASY

(I'd credit this list's source, but there are so many conflicting Google results, I can't accurately pinpoint the original source!)

You is such a powerful word, that even major social platforms use this strategy to create a subtle call to action and create a feeling of personalization .

Pinterest:

Tik Tok:

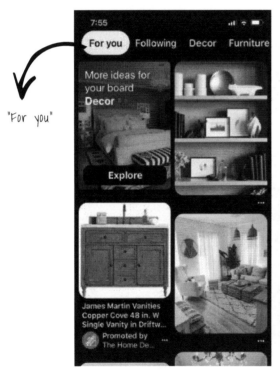

"For you"

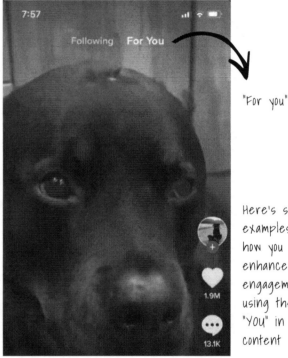

"For you"

Here's some examples showing how you can enhance your engagement by using the word "YOU" in your content

A special shout out to my dear friend Judi Fox who taught me the power of the word "You"

Connect with Judi on Linkedin **linkedin/.com/in/judiwfox** to learn more about writing content that converts! #foxrocks

EXAMPLES OF "I" VERSUS "YOU" CAPTIONS

"I" EXAMPLE

"My favorite song is Happy by Pharrell and I blast it every time I need to shake off a mood and get into the groove!

Last week I was speaking at a conference in Las Vegas and had the opportunity to pump up the crowd and of course played this song!"

The caption doesn't invite the reader into the story. It's a statement about your experience and your favorite song.

"YOU" EXAMPLE

7:59

CHELSEA.PEITZ
Posts

chelsea.peitz What song makes you get up and groove? I'm making the ultimate happy dance playlist and need your help! 💃 🕺

Wondering what jam made this photo op a reality? 🎤

Here's a clue:

"Ti esrever dna ti pilf, nwod gniht ym tup"

Drop your fav dance jams down below

This caption immediately asks the reader to participate by sharing their favorite song. The caption intros with a question and also tells the reader to comment below with their song. Two calls to action in this caption.

I'm crossing off one of my bucket list items! I can't wait to visit Italy and see all the things!!

This caption can be considered inspirational and sharing a personal story is an excellent way to create connections with your community, however, this caption could be improved

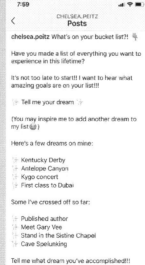

7:59

CHELSEA.PEITZ
Posts

chelsea.peitz What's on your bucket list?!

Have you made a list of everything you want to experience in this lifetime?

It's not too late to start!! I want to hear what amazing goals are on your list!!!

Tell me your dream

(You may inspire me to add another dream to my list)

Here's a few dreams on mine:

- Kentucky Derby
- Antelope Canyon
- Kygo concert
- First class to Dubai

Some I've crossed off so far:

- Published author
- Meet Gary Vee
- Stand in the Sistine Chapel
- Cave Spelunking

Tell me what dream you've accomplished!!!

This caption kicks off with a question nearly every reader has an answer for! It invites readers to join in and share.

2

COPYWRITING FORMULAS

These commonly used copywriting formulas have been sourced from this amazing article written by Kevan Lee for Buffer.com. For even more ideas, visit this link https://buffer.com/resources/copywriting-formulas

Copy is not written. Copy is assembled.
– Eugene Schwartz

WHAT TO SAY AND HOW TO SAY IT.

Coming up with a persuasive hook will help capture the reader's attention, but then it's up to the rest of your caption to keep it.

This is where copywriting formulas come into play!

Leading your reader from one sentence to the next means that you need to deliver on your promise, tell them a story they can relate to and also create tension that only you can solve.

Have no fear, because there are several well-known, proven copywriting formulas that can easily be applied to any industry. By following these templates, you will immediately improve your copy.

Whether you are creating an ad, an email blast, social post or blog, these "plug and play" formulas can help you organize and construct your content in a way that drives action and results.

1. BEFORE- AFTER- BRIDGE

Identify your ideal customer's challenges and then inspire them to imagine their lives with those problems being solved. The last section (your service or product) "bridges" the gap between the two worlds.

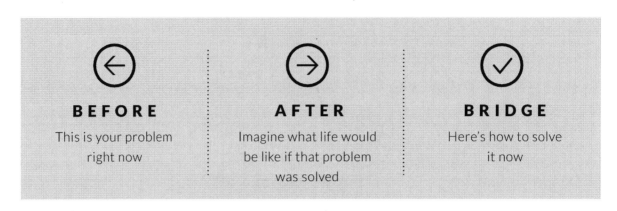

BEFORE

This is your problem right now

AFTER

Imagine what life would be like if that problem was solved

BRIDGE

Here's how to solve it now

EXAMPLE

Buying your first home.......... What if you could qualify for a home with zero money out of pocket! Find out how:

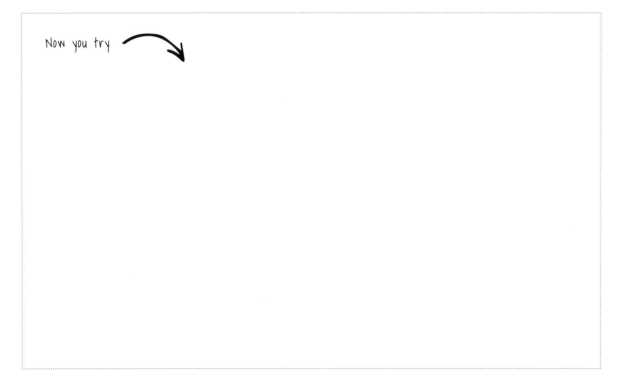

Now you try

2. PROBLEM – AGITATE – SOLVE

In this example, the problem doesn't get solved. Instead, the reader is encouraged to envision what happens if that problem exists (the agitate part). This formula focuses on creating empathy.

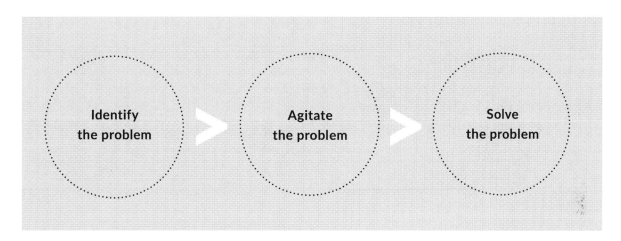

EXAMPLE

Selling your home can be stressful especially in a shifting market.

Your home is your biggest asset and holds your most important memories.

Selling your home without an expert can provide you some savings but will it give you piece of mind knowing that you're working with an experienced team that can help you sell in the least amount of time for the most amount of money.

Now you try

Problem Agitate Solve Formula created by Dan Kennedy, Copywriter

3. FEATURES - ADVANTAGES - BENEFITS

The focus in this formula is the benefit. This is the "results in" portion of the UVP formula outlined earlier in this workbook.

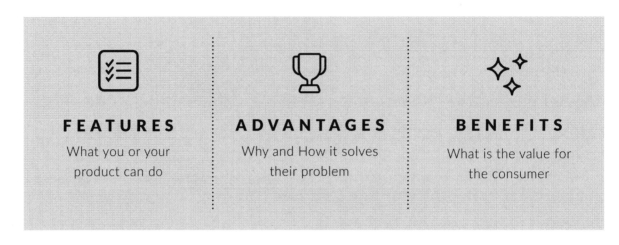

FEATURES
What you or your product can do

ADVANTAGES
Why and How it solves their problem

BENEFITS
What is the value for the consumer

EXAMPLE

Our Advanced Facebook Ad training is a step-by-step formula that anyone, regardless of skill level, can implement and execute!

Now you try

Features Advantages Benefits formula created by Joe Vitale
https://www.amazon.com/Hypnotic-Writing-Seduce-Persuade-Customers/dp/0470009799

4. THE 4 C'S FORMULA OR THE 4 U'S FORMULA

THE 4 C'S			
1. Clear Tell them exactly what they get	**2. Concise** Keep it short, sweet and to the point	**3. Compelling** Give them a reason to take action	**4. Credible** Prove your expertise

THE 4 U'S			
1. Useful Solves their problem	**2. Urgent** Take action now	**3. Unique** Your competitive advantage	**4. Ultra-Specific** Speaks to your niche

EXAMPLES

Going live on Instagram in 60 minutes to share all my secrets on generating more home buyer leads for under $100 per month!

This will NOT be replayed!

Webinar Wednesday is serving you up the top 3 mistakes you must avoid when purchasing your first investment property!

Limited spots – Register now!

Now you try

4 C's Formula created by Bob Bly https://articles.ibpa-online.org/article/a-new-copywriting-formula-the-4-cs/

4 U's Formula created by Michael Masterson http://www.michaelmasterson.net/whois.html

5. AIDA

ATTENTION

Jar the reader out of their boring ol' lives

INTEREST

Engage their mind with unusual, counter-intuitive or fresh info

DESIRE

Engage their heat so they will want what you are offering

ACTION

Ask them to take the next step

AIDA formula created by Elmo Lewis https://en.wikipedia.org/wiki/AIDA_(marketing)

EXAMPLE

A

I

D

A

🔑 We have put together a FREE list of homes for sale priced under $399,000 in the Happy Valley. Check out these listings! Perfect for first time home buyers and some of these homes even qualify for special financing programs.

Click HERE to view the... ✓ Learn More

Click HE view the.

👍 Like   💬 Comment

TravisThom.com

PRO TIP

Keep your audience reading by leading them into the next section with "teaser" sentences throughout your text.

EXAMPLES OF TEASERS

- *Here's what you need to know:*
- *Wanna learn how?*
- *So this happened...*
- *The secret:*
- *Advanced strategies*

- *I couldn't believe what I learned next*
- *Like this:*
- *Whoa!*
- *Let's get to it!*
- *You know what's awesome...*

(3)

CALLS TO ACTION (CTA)

Every piece of content you make (regardless of format) should include a call to action. It can be in the form of a simple question designed to elicit engagement or a command directing your audience to take action. Your audience needs to be told what to do and why to do it! I don't mean that offensively – by giving them a prompt to take an action, you're increasing your chances for more engagement which means more reach or possibly moving a potential lead into action.

TAKE ACTION, URGENCY, EXCLUSIVITY AND QUESTION CTAS

- Learn more
- Build
- Grow
- Discover
- Find
- Download
- Subscribe
- Click here
- Stop
- Try
- Join free/now
- Explore
- New Post
- Schedule a ....
- Enter now
- Pre-register
- Pre-order
- Talk to us now
- Get your free ....
- Become an expert
- Start
- Sign Up
- Let's connect
- Launch course

- Create account
- I'm ready!
- Let's chat
- Yes, Please!
- Find out more
- See what I'm up to
- Save time/money by
- Do you want more .... ?
- Immediately
- Instant
- Hurry!
- Last chance to
- Limited supply
- Only a few left
- Ends tomorrow
- Only available up to
- Limited time only
- One-time offer
- Expires soon

- Urgent
- Deadline is tonight
- While supplies last
- Special offer
- Invitation
- Limited Spots
- Members only
- Tell me ....
- What do you think?
- Do you agree with ...?
- Do you do this too?
- Tell me why you agree/ don't agree
- Which one of the above are you guilty of
- Why do we do this ...
- Would you rather ...?
- What is your favorite ...?
- True or false?

EXAMPLES

- *Download FREE list of homes now*

- *Discover how to save 10% on your purchase*

- *Start your home search here*

- *Click here to get your home valuation*

- *Get your FREE market update*

- *Last chance to grab your spot at our community Fall Festival this Friday!*

- *Hurry! Grab your FREE......*

- *Instant home valuation*

- *Know someone who needs to know about ......?*

- *What do you think about ....?*

PRO TIP:

Your audio and video content should also include a verbal call to action.
Example: Subscribe to this podcast, Click the link in the description to grab your FREE download

CAPTION DO'S SUMMARY

- Focus on a specific customer avatar and envision them as you write

- Use an attention grabbing first sentence (think news and blog headlines!)

- Tell a story that brings your audience into the journey and start off your copy with a "hook"

- Speak to one reader/viewer by using the word "YOU" not "I", "we" or "our." By using the word "you," the content or story becomes about the consumer and not about your brand. By addressing your audience personally, ("you"), they begin to see themselves in the story and it also makes the post more shareable, because it's not about you.

- Include a call to action to encourage engagement, drive traffic and generate leads (can be at the beginning, middle or end and also a combination of those!)

- Don't allow your content to become "clickbait." Give them the goods they came to access and make it frictionless, one-click and easy to access

- Optimize your content's readability by formatting your copy for the "social skim" - Short, one or two sentence paragraphs rather than large blocks of content

- Using short sentence fragments is encouraged (ex: "And then I knew."/ "That was it.")

- Use a casual, conversational tone (write like you talk)

- Write in a jargon free, easy to understand language and avoid industry specific lingo

- Be concise – remove extra words (ex "can" vs. "exhibits the ability to")

- Use simple words (ex: "help" vs. "assist"/ "get rid of" vs. "eliminate")

- Use words that appeal to human emotion

- You're able to use contractions (see what I did there)

- It's okay to end your sentences with a preposition in casual text (ex: "This is someone you should talk with")

- Starting your sentences with "And, Or, For and But" are totally okay

- Use correct spellings (ex: night vs nite or though vs tho) - unless for effect

- It's ok to use emojis in your copy but don't use so many that your copy looks like hieroglyphics and stops the normal flow of reading

- Using hashtags on social platforms is encouraged but avoid using #hashtags #throughout your #copy because it #makes it #harder to #read

- Talk with your audience, not at them

- Ask your audience question(s) to increase engagement and comments

- Understand the difference between features and benefits – the benefits are the important parts and typically solve the customer's problem

- Read everything you write out loud before publishing

- Consider adding captions to video content to increase engagement and allow those watching without sound to easily consume your content

EMPOWER YOUR ALGORITHMS

"Reach is arguably the most valuable non-monetary asset in the world. OK, so if it's so valuable, what is "reach" and why is it so valuable? Reach is the ability to influence large groups of people. It's the capacity to connect with and influence hundreds, thousands, hundreds of thousands and even millions of people. Reach is what Michael Jordan has. It's what Oprah has. It's what Warren Buffet has. It's what every single successful person in the 21st-century is going to HAVE to have if they expect any modicum of success. It's a connected world, and it expects you to be connected too."

Keenan, Author Not Taught

THE FACEBOOK ALGORITHM EXPLAINED

Maximizing your reach means optimizing your content for the algorithms.

Algorithms are step-by-step mathematical instructions that are used for data processing, automated reasoning and predicting which Netflix series you might want to see next. They are neither good nor evil.

Generally speaking, algorithms are a good thing because they help us spend our time seeing the content and creators we're interested in seeing first and more often. It makes our lives easier by saving us time and making the systems we use smarter.

Algorithms are how The Socials sort content for you. These "smart" programs learn what you like based on your behaviors (connections, likes, comments, shares, searches and views) and then serves up content it predicts that you want to see first.

While we don't control the algorithms, understanding how they work and what signals they are looking for and rewarding, you can help your content go farther (more reach) and get seen by the right people more often (better engagement).

In this section, I focus only on Facebook and Instagram because the majority of you are using these two platforms and both companies have publicly outlined what signals their algorithms are weighting and tracking.

While each Social has its own unique algorithm, the best practices covered in this section can positively impact your content's performance on all of the platforms.

FACEBOOK'S ALGORITHM PROMOTES CONTENT THAT:

| Connects people | Sparks conversation | Is informative, inspiring or entertaining | Is memorable, authentic and enduring | Builds community |

In January 2018, Facebook announced a *"major ranking change"* that focused on **"meaningful interactions"**.

"Meaningful Interactions"

1. Commenting
2. Sharing
3. Direct messages
4. Time Spent reading content or viewing a video

The Offical Facebook Statement:

"Today we use signals like how many people react to, comment on or share posts to determine how high they appear in News Feed. With this update, we will also prioritize posts that spark conversations and meaningful interactions between people. To do this, we will predict which posts you might want to interact with your friends about, and show these posts higher in feed. These are posts that inspire back-and-forth discussion in the comments and posts that you might want to share and react to – whether that's a post from a friend seeking advice, a friend asking for recommendations for a trip, or a news article or video prompting lots of discussion."

> **"We will also prioritize posts from friends and family over public content, consistent with our News Feed Values."***

*NOTE: If you're wondering if this means your Business Page content isn't going to go as far, you're right. Facebook's algorithm favors content shared from a Personal Timeline. Here's the skinny directly from Facebook's founder:

> **"We started making changes in this direction last year, but it will take months for this new focus to make its way through all our products. The first changes you'll see will be in News Feed, where you can expect to see more from your friends, family and groups. As we roll this out, you'll see less public content like posts from businesses, brands, and media. And the public content you see more will be held to the same standard --it should encourage meaningful interactions between people."****

This doesn't mean you should abandon your Business Page. It does mean that you need to focus on creating quality content that provides value or entertainment and also consider a paid strategy to promote Page content for more reach.

*Source: https://newsroom.fb.com/news/2018/01/news-feed-fyi-bringing-people-closer-together/
**Source: Mark Zuckerberg https://newsroom.fb.com/news/2018/01/news-feed-fyi-bringing-people-closer-together/

CONTENT RANKING FACTORS

Representatives from Buffer.com attended an exclusive Facebook News Feed webinar for publishers and shared the details in a comprehensive blog post.

In simple terms, Facebook's algorithm uses the following four components to provide a positive user experience which includes seeing relevant content from the accounts you care about most.

Top 4 Content Ranking Factors:

1 **Inventory** (what content is available)

2 **Signals** (content freshness, format, publisher intent ie educate, entertain etc, relationship to poster)

Most important

3 **Predictions** (what's the likelihood that the user will have a positive interaction with a specific content piece)

4 **Overall Score** (A score assigned by a combination of the above that determines what content you see)

https://buffer.com/resources/facebook-algorithm

Facebook now ranks content heavily by the amount of "active" versus "passive" interactions it receives.

Facebook is even weighting longer comments over short comments or a single emoji response.

Active interactions such as sharing, commenting, and reacting will hold much more weight than "passive" interactions such as clicking, viewing, or hovering.

ACTIVE INTERACTIONS VS. PASSIVE INTERACTIONS

Source: Buffer.com

Active (Positive)	Passive (Neutral)
⌃ Commenting	⊖ Clicking
⌃ Sharing	⊖ Watching
⌃ Reacting	⊖ Viewing / Hovering

"So one of the key things is understanding what types of interactions people find meaningful, what inspires them to interact more or share more in the future. Some of the specific things would be like we're going to be (weighing) long comments more than short comments, because we find regularly that if you take the time to actually write a more thoughtful perspective on something that correlates positively with a comment that someone actually would respond to or Like. It also correlates negatively with problematic content types like spam or uncivil content, et cetera."

Adam Mosseri

WHAT CONTENT DOES
THE ALGORITHM FAVOR?

Does Facebook "prefer" one content format over another?

———

If you're making quality content that's valuable to your audience, the format of that content isn't as critical as the message you're communicating. However, Facebook has directly stated that it's algorithm favors video content.

(This doesn't mean that photos or text content isn't valuable or may not get as much reach! Good content is good content!)

Native video, or video content that is uploaded directly into the platform versus shared from YouTube or another video hosting site, outperforms. The Socials want to be the original source for your content and do not want to send users away from their platforms to view a piece of content. Sharing is caring, but not when it comes to your video posts.

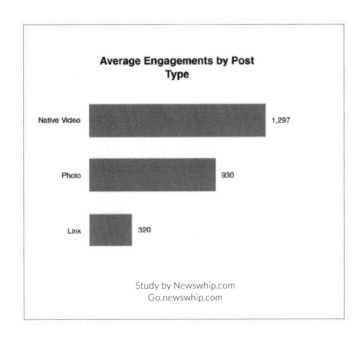

Average Engagements by Post Type

Native Video — 1,297
Photo — 930
Link — 320

Study by Newswhip.com
Go.newswhip.com

Many people ask me if Facebook ranks content by format and while I can't locate a statement directly from Facebook on this topic, here's anecdotally what I've noticed with my own posts:

Content Performance

1. Live Video

2. Short Recorded Vertical Video

3. Status Update Question with Color Background

4. Single Image with Text

** Link posts do NOT typically get as much reach and engagement. Sharing an article as a post may underperform because it sends users off of the platform when clicked on. If you do come across an awesome article, apply the 3 T's and create your OWN original content!

LIVE VIDEO TIPS

Facebook Live video posts receive 6x more engagement than any other kind of post
- Facebook.com

Benefits of Live Video:
- Better community real time engagement = more human relationships
- Notifications are sent to followers when live
- Preferred Story feed placement
- You can go live with another person without being in the same location

BEST PRACTICES FOR LIVE (AND ALSO RECORDED) VIDEO CONTENT:

Get Prepped:

- Prepare with some ideas or bullets to keep you on track but don't read from a teleprompter or memorize a script. People want to feel as though you are communicating with them in a natural casual tone, as you would with friends or family. You may want to write down a few questions in advance that you could ask the audience to create some engagement.

- Plan for your surroundings. Find a location preferably with decent lighting (or come prepared with a clip on ring light for your smartphone) and without a lot of visual distractions or background noise. If you plan to stream in public, consider bringing earbuds or a mic to plug into your phone with a built in mic or a lav mic. Keep in mind, when you are Live in public, you should remain cognizant of other people's desire for privacy who may not want to be filmed.

- Double check yourself and your surroundings. Is there anything in the background you wouldn't want people to see? How about your clothing? Can people tell you're wearing your pajama bottoms (and watch out for reflections LOL). You would be amazed at what viewers notice!

- Many people like to have fun and play music in the background – while showing your personality is key, just remember, Facebook is able to "hear" music played in the background and adheres to copyright laws meaning, they may not allow you to post your live video if it includes music that is under copyright. It may not happen every time, but it has happened and you can be locked out of your account for a period of time for repeated offenses. It's a good idea to place a disclaimer in your live description area that says the following : *"disclaimer: I do not own the rights to music or sounds played during this live"*

- Make sure you have a solid wifi connection, write a compelling description for the video and decide who will see the video (public, friends lists etc)

- If you are planning on walking and talking, consider using a small tripod to hold the phone as it will help with the fluidity of the video and try not to move too quickly as it will be harder for your audience to watch.

- Pre-market your Live streams to let people know when they can tune in. Post to your social channels and send emails a day or two before going Live to build anticipation and give followers enough time to tune in.

  You can use the Facebook Premiere option on any Facebook Business Page to schedule a pre-recorded video that will receive the same benefits as a live video. Basically, you can upload a video and it will "premiere" as if it were actually live. When setting up a Premiere, a post is created for your Page that announces the upcoming live stream where viewers can sign up for reminders. Using this option also allows you to post your video to Facebook Watch, a separate tab within Facebook that acts like YouTube showcasing user videos and original programming. By doing so, your video may see increased reach.

- Mirror your phone if you are using a white board. Keep in mind, viewers are going to see things in reverse or mirror mode, so if you have an example such as a white board or easil with paper you are writing on, be sure to turn your camera to mirror mode before hitting live (Tap the magic wand icon in the Live settings section, then go to Tools and Select the flip icon)

Go Live:

- Look into the actual camera, not your own eyes in the screen of the phone. It will feel strange at first, but eye contact is the key to building a connection.

- As uncomfortable as it may feel in the beginning, appearing with a smile and energy can really make a difference for those who are watching. It may feel a bit unnatural at first, but being a bit more over-animated than you think is important to make your audience feel like you have energy! Bring up your energy one notch higher without being over the top - energy and facial expressions are contagious and we may feel like we're acting a little over the top but it may not come across like that on the camera.

- If you use your laptop or desktop, your live video will be horizontal. Vertical appears bigger in the feed and is the preferred viewing aspect for most users these days. It can make it a bit more difficult if you want to repurpose the video on a platform due to the different sizing requirements. IGTV, Facebook Stories & Instagram Stories are all vertical.

- Introduce yourself – if you have a tagline or UVP that you KNOW by heart and feel comfortable saying then include that as well! Keep intro very short – 10-15 seconds max.

FROM LIVE STREAM EXPERT TRISH LETO TRISHLETO.COM
The first 30 seconds cover your who, what, why, and how:

- **Who are you?**
  State your name, company and UVP

- **What are you talking about?**
  Hook em in and tease the topic

- **Why should we watch?**
  Why the topic is important to the VIEWER not why you want to talk about it

- **How do we get more of your content?**
  Give them a call to action and direction on what to do next (put a sticky note on your computer to remind you!)

- If you get an incoming call during your Live, just hit decline and your Live will continue as normal. Consider turning on Do Not Disturb on your phone (but don't forget to turn it off afterwards!)

- Sometimes there could be a delay or you could see that viewers are watching but you aren't able to see their names yet. Eventually, they should appear.

- Tell your viewers to subscribe to your Live Notifications so they can be notified every time you go Live.

- If you have a guest joining you to go live via third party software it's always a good idea to test with the guest before going live as technical difficulties do happen!

- If you see people joining you live, take the time to quickly say hello, but try not to get into a side conversation unless you are specifically asking people questions during the live broadcast. People who are tuning in and want to take in the information you are sharing may not want to be interrupted multiple times for personal asides or constant hellos. Most of your views will be replays and they don't want to waste time!

- Never drive and go live. It's not safe and it's not good for your personal brand.

After Your Live:
- Edit your video and optimize it by changing the thumbnail if you desire, location, date, provide a longer description and even select a category.

- Add subtitles for those watching without sound (yes, most Facebook videos are in fact watched without sound unless the viewer actively clicks on the video) Facebook Business Pages will autogenerate captions for you in the editing section of the video itself.

- Respond to all of your comments and focus on actual replies not just likes if possible, it shows that you took the time to type an actual response to those who took the time to watch you.

- Experiment with time of day AM, Noon, PM to see when you have more viewers. Don't let this prevent you from being consistent. It's better to go Live often than to only go Live within a self-imposed time restriction that you may miss.

- Check your metrics on Business Page live videos to review watchtime and where viewers drop off and determine if you can improve or change your tactics moving forward.

- Typically, live streams on a personal profile get more engagement and viewership than business pages. You can always repurpose some or all of your live video onto other Pages and you can tag or share your live video from personal profile to your business Page. If you want to create a Facebook ad in the future, it's a good idea to host some live broadcasts FROM your Business Page and then share to your personal. The reason for this is as follows: When you originate a live video on your Business Page, Facebook will track the viewers and allow you to build a custom audience to whom you can serve ads in the future. You won't have this option if you originate on your Personal Profile.

MAY 2019 FACEBOOK VIDEO ALGORITHM UPDATES

Directly sourced from Facebook for Media blog

The following pages in this section were directly sourced and quoted from Facebook's Newsroom and Media Blogs - sources at end of chapter.

These are not new principles, but we will be strengthening their influence among the multiple factors that determine video distribution.
-Facebook

FACEBOOK VIDEO RANKING ALGORITHM FACTORS

1. Originality

Facebook is focused on promoting authentic, valuable content and prioritizes video content that has strong "signals of originality." These signals include:

- **Sharing videos that you wrote, shot, edited and published yourself or with the support of a production partner.**

THINGS THAT MAY HURT YOUR ORIGINALITY SIGNAL AND LIMIT DISTRIBUTION AND MONETIZATION FOR YOUR VIDEOS ARE:

- **Posting duplicate content.**
  Posting content that already exists on Facebook or that has been posted somewhere else first and which you had no meaningful role in creating. (Reposting content you made yourself, however, is fine.)

- **Posting mass-produced or repurposed clips** Posting footage from others that has not been meaningfully transformed and appears to have been stitched together with little enhancement.

  Facebook's focus on originality is primarily aimed at Pages that have paid arrangements to "inauthentically" share content

2. "Loyalty" and "Intent

When people regularly come back to view a creator's videos, Facebook views that as a strong, positive signal for distribution. This is especially true when people actively search for your content or seek it out on video-first destinations like Facebook Watch or directly on your Page.

YOU CAN ENCOURAGE THESE BEHAVIORS FOR YOUR VIDEOS BY:

- **Optimizing your content for Facebook search**.
  This includes writing clear titles and descriptions for your posts and including a few relevant tags. This can help more people see your content, both via Search results and also via the recommended videos that we show to people in News Feed and in Facebook Watch.

- **Publishing "bonus" content**
  Like Live videos, photos, or text posts to stay connected with your fans and deepen engagement in between publishing longer videos. This means not only posting one type of post and using a variety of posting formats.

- **Loyalty = repeat viewers**

- **Intent = viewers directly search for your name or Page name by typing it into the search bar or go directly to your Page to watch videos.**

NOTE: You can also use the FREE website Creator Studio to check insights such as Loyalty and Intent for any of your Business Pages. Log in here: ***https://business.facebook.com/creatorstudio***

- Track viewing behaviors at the Page level via **Loyalty Insights > How Long People Are Watching**.

- Track viewing behaviors at the video level via **Performance Insights > [Select a video] > Post Performance > Audience Retention.**

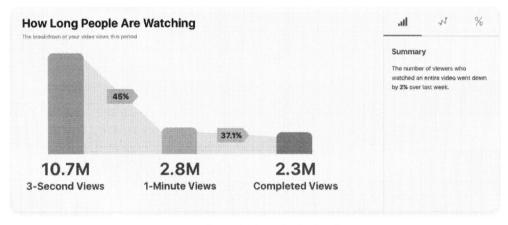

Image credit: Facebook.com/facebookmedia

- FB Watch and IGTV promote longer form, episodic content. Consider creating a consistently scheduled series with themed content. Post weekly on the same day.

- Create a weekly/monthly content calendar to stay prepared and consistent.

- Preview your videos on Facebook using the "Premiere" option.

- Host a "Facebook Watch Party" which is a new way for people to watch videos on Facebook together in real time. A Watch Party is a Group feature that allows Group Admins to hold a live screening of a pre-recorded video where Group members can comment in real time as they watch.

- Create "Playlists" for your Business Page videos to promote "bingeable" content. "Playlists" let you organize videos into groups based on common themes or topics that encourage viewers to "binge" on your content.

- Include a verbal call to action during your video that tells viewers about your weekly schedule and when to tune in to encourage repeat viewership.

- Include comprehensive video descriptions and titles that include relevant keywords.

- Use higher quality video; no slideshows. A slideshow is a series of still images that are animated to appear to be more video-like but are not an actual video.

3. Video Length

Facebook is not only looking at the length of your videos but also reviews the length of time people are watching and if they view the entire video and engage with it by commenting, saving and sharing.

- **Make longer videos that engage people and inspire them to watch to the end.**
  Research has shown that people on Facebook find value in longer videos that have a storyline. Facebook prioritizes longer videos **(three minutes or more)** that inspire people to continue watching. So be sure to plan your video's opening, build-up, tension, pacing and payoff in ways that will catch a viewer's attention and hold it until the end.

- **Video watch time:**
  1 minute or more and bonus points for completion. This means creating an outline and a "hook" with calls to action will be critical to maintaining viewer attention.

4. No "Engagement Baiting"

Nobody likes clickbait and Facebook has ways to detect and demote artificial attempts to boost watch times by exaggerating details and omitting crucial information.

Facebook is not only reading your video description text but also listening for engagement baiting phrases such as: **"comment below", "tag a friend" or "share this"**

DIRECTLY SOURCED FROM FACEBOOK MEDIA BLOG:

"We prioritize content that sparks conversations and meaningful interactions between real people. To do this, we increase distribution for videos that inspire friend-to-friend or person-to-person interactions.

VIDEOS THAT DO THIS WELL WILL:

- **Inspire people to have meaningful, back and forth, respectful discussion in the comments.** This has to happen in a way that is not spammy or gratuitous.

- **Be authentically shared.** Shares remain one of Facebook's most powerful tools for organic distribution.

- **Be engaged with.** We also look at likes and reactions to help us determine which content should get distribution priority. These interactions should happen organically and not through engagement bait.

VIDEOS MAY FACE REDUCED DISTRIBUTION IF THEY:

- **Employ manufactured sharing behaviors.** This is when a Page's content is artificially distributed through re-shares or sharing within a group, usually in exchange for compensation. Examples of this are when a Page repeatedly shares content from another Page with which they have no direct connection, and the content is not related to any theme of their Page.

- **Resort to engagement bait.** This is when a Page resorts to tactics for vote baiting, tag baiting, share baiting, comment baiting, react baiting. Posts that ask people to engage in order to win a prize or vote on a topic are good examples of engagement baiting content that will earn less distribution on our platform.

PRO TIPS

- Avoid asking viewers to respond in specific ways. Specifically instructing viewers to "like", "tag", or "share" may result in your content being flagged for engagement baiting.

- When asking for feedback in the description and comments, use questions that allow for a wide range of responses. Questions that have predefined answers - eg. "What's your address birth month?" - are more likely to be flagged as baiting.

- Give conversation-starters, not instructions. Instead of telling viewers exactly what to say or how to say it, invite them to share their thoughts, general feedback and questions.

- Use the post's description field as intended. Tell viewers about yourself and your content. Share the link to your page and let viewers know what they can expect if they choose to follow you.

SocialInsider.io recently analyzed over 9,036,594 of video posts from a total of 92k business pages from a variety of categories and sizes.

THEIR RESEARCH SHOWED THE FOLLOWING:

- Facebook Video is NOT fully saturated; there is still room for your video content!

- Vertical Video is the most used video format & also the top performing

- 300 word video text descriptions have the highest average number of interactions (that's approximately two sentences).

- In comparison with other types of video (landscape, square), vertical video appears to impact significantly on the number of people watching a video, the duration of the viewing, and their willingness to engage with it.

- The optimal length of Facebook Video on Pages of all sizes was 2-5 minutes in length

- Videos that succeed on Facebook are dynamic and take full advantage of the format's capabilities. Videos that rely too heavily on static images can have their distribution reduced.

https://www.socialinsider.io/blog/facebook-video-study/

Further reading on Facebook updates:

2017 updates:
- www.facebook.com/facebookmedia/blog/updates-to-video-distribution-and-monetization/
- newsroom.fb.com/news/2017/12/news-feed-fyi-for-video-intent-repeat-viewership-matter/

2018 updates:
- www.facebook.com/facebookmedia/blog/best-practices-and-updates-on-video-and-monetization
- www.facebook.com/facebookmedia/blog/video-best-practices
- www.facebook.com/facebookmedia/blog/understanding-video-distribution-on-facebook

2019 updates:
- newsroom.fb.com/news/2019/05/updates-to-video-ranking/

THE INSTAGRAM
ALGORITHM EXPLAINED

"Instagram relies on machine learning based on your past behavior to create a unique feed for everyone. Even if you follow the exact same accounts as someone else, you'll get a personalized feed based on how you interact with those accounts.

The order of photos and videos in your feed will be based on the likelihood you'll be interested in the content, your relationship with the person posting and the timeliness of the post"

- Instagram's Product Lead, Julian Gutman June 2018

How does the algorithm work?

At a very basic level, Instagram's algorithm shows you content that it predicts you will want to see based on your past behaviors, accounts you follow and who you talk to.

If you like an accounts posts often or send direct messages to the same account repeatedly, it will 'learn' that you want to see more of this account's content.

If you engage with cooking posts or dog posts, you'll see more of that type of content in your Explore tab.

If someone you follow has a post that receives a high level of engagement, you may see that post higher in your feed. If your post receives engagement (comments, likes, shares, bookmarks) then it signals to the algorithm that the post is valuable in some way and should be put in more people's feeds (reach).

THE 6 FACTORS OF THE INSTAGRAM ALGOTHRIM

Interest

- What you see is based on who you follow and what you like
- It relies on past behavior to create a unique feed for everyone
- Even if you follow the same accounts as your friend, you both won't see the exact same feeds

Timeliness

- How long ago the post was made. Newer seen more often.
- Instagram's goal is to show you fresh content which means the algorithm will prioritize recent posts.

Relationship

- Instagram wants to show you content from the people you care about (friends and family categories) and in order to determine who those people are, they will look at your engagement with accounts. Indicators of close relationship include: Commenting, DM'ing, Tagging, Turning on Notifications for posts.

Frequency

How often you open and use the app. If you check in a lot, then you may see more of a chronological feed because Instagram wants to show you the best posts since you last checked it. If you don't open it a lot, then Instagram will serve you content that it thinks you may like versus the above.

Following

If you follow a lot of people, you have more content to see so it's not likely you'll see every post from every account in your feed.

Usage (session time)

If you spend a lot of time in the app, then you'll see more posts because Instagram is trying to serve up content it knows you want to see. If you only check it once a day, they will serve you up the best of the best based on what it thinks you want to see.

This is a direct extract from the article Instagram Mythbusting from TechCrunch
https://techcrunch.com/2018/06/01/how-instagram-feed-works/

INSTAGRAM ALGORITHM MYTHS BUSTED

The following list is sourced from a TechCrunch interview in which Instagram executives directly debunked common Instagram myths:

- Instagram is not at this time considering an option to see the old reverse chronological feed because it doesn't want to add more complexity (users might forget what feed they're set to), but it is listening to users who dislike the algorithm.

- Instagram does not hide posts in the feed, and you'll see everything posted by everyone you follow if you keep scrolling.

- Feed ranking does not favor the photo or video format universally, but people's feeds are tuned based on what kind of content they engage with, so if you never stop to watch videos you might see fewer of them.

- Instagram's feed doesn't favor users who use Stories, Live, or other special features of the app.

- Instagram doesn't downrank users for posting too frequently or for other specific behaviors, but it might swap in other content in between someone's if they rapid-fire separate posts.

- Instagram doesn't give extra feed presence to personal accounts or business accounts, so switching won't help your reach.

- Shadowbanning is not a real thing, and Instagram says it doesn't hide people's content for posting too many hashtags or taking other actions.

This is a direct extract from the article Instagram Mythbusting from TechCrunch
https://techcrunch.com/2018/06/01/how-instagram-feed-works/

Stop Complicating Content - *Let's make this easy and straight to the point*

ENERGIZE YOUR ENGAGEMENT

"Going viral is not an outcome;
it's a happening. Sometimes it happens;
sometimes it doesn't. Just remember,
fans are vanity and sales are sanity."

Lori Taylor, Advertising Exec

ENERGIZE YOUR ENGAGEMENT

Better Engagement = More Reach = More Brand Awareness = More Results

As you've already learned from the previous chapter, the algorithms are rewarding "meaningful" interactions aka engagement. Content pushing and conversation starting are two completely different things. The act of posting content alone isn't going to drive conversions – it's the context of your content and your community's conversations that generates results.

This chapter will teach you tried and true engagement boosting tips that will make you and your content work smarter, not harder.

ENGAGEMENT CHELSEA-ISMS

↘ Faces take you places:
   Show your face, create a connection & accelerate trust

↘ Teach before you reach
   Share value, give and teach before you ask for anything

↘ Don't stalk unless you talk
   Comments are currency to your algorithm & audience- don't be a lurker

↘ Let your comments be your content
   It's likely your best content, it supports others and brands you as a Superfan

↘ Consistency doesn't have to mean daily
   Focus on quality not quantity

(more Chelsea-isms at the end of this book☺)

ENGAGEMENT DONT'S

BUY LIKES OR FOLLOWERS

Yes, you can easily Google online services that promise to grow your social media following, however, it's highliy unlikely that these accounts will convert to customers and may not even be a real person. The algorithms 'know' if your account receives a sudden spike in followers and can track inauthentic activity. The FTC ruled in Oct 2019 that the "sale of fake indicators of social media influence" is illegal.

USE 3RD PARTY "BOTS" TO LIKE/COMMENT/FOLLOW/UNFOLLOW

Typically, these third party automation tools violate social media platforms' terms of service. You could be blocked from accessing your accounts and may never be able to regain access. Nobody likes inauthentic engagement AND more importantly, simply downloading certain unapproved apps that connect to Instagram could get your account action blocked for a period of time.

SET UP AUTO-RESPONDER SYSTEMS WITH GENERIC COMMENTS

Most consumers find these canned messages impersonal and annoying. If an auto-response is perceived as spammy or doesn't fit within the context of the current conversation, it could negatively impact your brand (and get you reported as spam or blocked).

SPAM PEOPLE VIA DIRECT MESSAGES

Sending someone a sales pitch as your first contact or immediately after following someone is poor social media etiquette and is an excellent way to be reported or blocked. If you are reported too many times, you can lose access to your account. Direct messages are very personal and should be intentional and human.

POST ONLY BUSINESS CONTENT

Customers want to relate to and connect with people who share common interests. With access to virtually any information online, it's more important to create content with value at its core. Being relevant and relatable are the keys to creating trust and credibility.

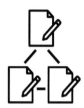

CROSS-POST ALL OF THE SAME CONTENT ACROSS MULTIPLE CHANNELS AT THE SAME TIME

The algorithms and your audience reward quality content over quantity. Posting less often but still consistently and with a higher quality post could help increase your reach and brand visibility. There's no set magic number for posting frequency. Stories are designed for frequent and daily micro content posts. The Feeds are not. Focus more on creating 1-2 high quality posts per week and committing to a consistent schedule.

OUTSOURCE ALL SOCIAL MEDIA POSTS/ CONTENT

While there are some cases in which hiring an outside company can be helpful in achieving your marketing efforts, social media is personal and social which means any company you hire would best serve your brand by offering personal and custom content that showcases your culture and or specific personal expertise.

POST ONLY "EVERGREEN"OR GENERIC CONTENT

Hyperlocal and hyper-relevant content is key. Gone are the days of posting generic house cleaning tips and expecting to see any engagement. Think about what matters to your ideal client and craft quality content over quantity.

POST AND GHOST:

The Socials "watch" the first hour of your post to determine if it should be shown to more people. The engagement a post receives within that critical time frame signals the algorithm to show that post to more people.

It's important to get active before you post and also stay active afterwards to reply to comments. You can't "post and ghost" and expect to get more reach because being a good community member means talking with your superfans. This doesn't mean you have to constantly refresh your feed and stare at the screen waiting to reply within seconds, but it does mean that you should check in regularly and turn your notifications on!

SOCIAL SHORT CUTS

Social short cuts are what I call tapping the heart, emoji reactions and the like button as you scroll down the Feeds. It's not your fault - Instagram makes it so easy to double tap a photo and those emojis are so cute it's hard to resist, but we should! Those quick-hitter actions are not really for the Creator, rather, they are for us – to validate that we've supported someone else and to feel like we accomplished engaging for the day. And, let's face it, we're lazy.

Comments and shares are for the content creator. With every comment, you're supporting and connecting with that person. You're also branding yourself because they see your pro-file photo and name with each notification and comment. Taking the time to write a sen-tence or even two shows them that you care and also trains the algorithm in your favor.

OVER-POST ON SOCIAL ACCOUNTS

One to two relevant posts per day is just fine, you don't want to clutter feeds with multiple posts – if you love to post, consider keeping that to Instagram Stories, Facebook Stories or Snapchat.

BE CAUTIOUS OF WHAT YOU COMMENT ON AND WHAT POSTS YOU LIKE.

Commenting on politics, religion or hot topics could be potential landmines. Also, consider changing your privacy settings for your personal profile timeline and tagging settings to ensure that you approve anything before it's shared to your timeline.

STEAL SOMEONE'S CONTENT

Don't use someone's content without including the appropriate credit. Being inspired by someone else's content is totally acceptable and by tagging that person you could generate additional engagement and potentially create a relationship!

OVERTAG PEOPLE

It's like being in a huge group text with endless update notifications. Be strategic and intentional with any direct communication. Personalization is the new black.

IGNORE COMMENTS

These are the lifeblood of algorithms – checking at least once per day and replying to all comments is a must do!

PRO TIPS

- Limit requests of "like my page" or "please share" as they can be viewed as spammy. Make good content and people will like and share without you having to ask.

- Be cognizant of how hashtags should be used and not used (or overused). Unless it's for comedic effect, only use one to three word phrases max for a hashtag for easy reading.

Now that we have the DONTS out of the way, let's focus on the DOS

THE ABCS OF ENGAGEMENT

A – AUTHENTICITY

This is one of my least favorite words because it's overused and under-explained. Relatability is the cornerstone of content that connects. Showing your face and using your voice are the foundations of humanizing content. Simply put, authenticity means showing your personality, your quirks, your sense of humor and your talents.

Your potential customers need to like you before they can trust you. Real life content helps your audience feel like they know you without even meeting you in person. Whether you like it or not, your face is now your brand and it's not about vanity or ego – it's simply about communicating in the most human way possible – eye to eye, screen to screen at a literal arm's length. The Socials even have patented facial recognition software which sounds creepy but proves that faces matter.

Sharing your own personal story is one of the very few things we can do at scale for FREE with a device we already own.

Authenticity beats an algorithm every time.

B – BOOKMARKS

Create highly shareable and saveable content to increase your engagement.

The algorithms sort and rank your content based on user behaviors like watch time, read time and saving or bookmarking posts. These actions indicate that your content is valuable and should be shown to more people.

Almost all social platforms offer a save, bookmark or watch later feature that allows you to save a post and organize them into folders or collections. These saved posts are not visible to the public but The Socials are tracking them.

There's a major caveat here – your content needs to be 'bookmark worthy' (or screenshot worthy if it's in a Story). Sharing a personal story about your holiday travels isn't as save worthy, unless you share your travel tips or best places to visit.

Examples of share-worthy content:
- Slide decks (presentations)
- Inspirational quotes
- Tips/Hacks
- How to's/Tutorials

PRO TIP

Add a call to action to your save-worthy content in the caption:
"save this post" or "bookmark this post so you can find it later."

C - CAPTIONS

85% of Facebook videos are watched without sound.

Adding captions to your video content increases its accessibility, discoverability and engagement.

"Research shows that 80% of consumers watch videos with captions to the end, compared to only 40% for videos without captions. Internal testing completed by Facebook also confirmed that adding captions to videos increases the average time viewed by 12%" – CoVideo.com

Captions provide users who are unable to hear or who choose not to turn on the volume the ability to consume your content. Captions also improve the SEO (search engine optimization) of your content because search engines like Google and YouTube "read" the captions to identify keywords to fulfill your search query.

By adding captions, you can increase your watch time which triggers the algorithm and boosts your post to more viewers and it shows higher in search engine results.

Most captioning services can also easily transcribe your audio or video content which allows you to easily re-purpose content to additional formats.

CAPTIONING TOOLS: Apple Clips app, Rev.com, Temi.com, RePurpose.io

PRO TIP

Adding text to your Facebook/Instagram Stories not only provides context to viewers but also stops the tapping as our brain slows down to read and creates more engagement.

D - DIRECT MESSAGES

Conversations lead to conversions.

While public comment sections on a post can lead to conversations, chances are private messaging will create exponentially more opportunity to go deeper with your community.
Imagine posting an educational video on Facebook about how to sell your house during a divorce. Do you think your community members will feel comfortable enough to talk about their personal divorce in the comments or more so in a one-to-one direct message?

Only 10 years ago, you needed someone's address, phone number or email to communicate with them. Today, thanks to free social networks, we don't even have to be a 'connection' or 'friend' to send someone a direct message (DM).

The algorithms are, in fact, 'watching' your Direct Message communication and ranks them as positive behavior. Does that mean if you are a heavy DM'er your content in the Feed will go farther? Maybe! Possibly! Probably!

This is why the Stories format is THE best place to create relationships – camera first, message enabled and real time. Remember, the more you DM with someone, the more often they see your content in the Feeds.

DMs are SACRED SPACE!

DO NOT, I repeat DO NOT pitch your products or services in the DM. Will someone respond to your sales pitch? Sure - it's a numbers game and sometimes you win but most of the time you will lose. If you're sending cold spam or even somewhat salesy sounding DMs, you're still going to annoy people. If you are reported as spam or blocked, that has a negative impact on your reach.

Make it your goal to send a minimum of 3-5 strategic Direct Messages per week day. If you did this for an entire year, you would have initiated 780 – 1300+ conversations per year. Imagine if only 1% of those conversations became a conversion!

PRO TIP

Send VOICE messages in the DM so people can hear your tone! Tap the microphone icon in your Facebook, Instagram or LinkedIn message to record.

E - ENGAGEMENT STICKERS FOR STORIES

Using (what I call) 'engagement stickers' on your Facebook and Instagram Stories is a fun and easy way to encourage your audience to engage without requiring them to send you a direct message. (Yes, the algorithms are also 'watching' to see if you're using these stickers!)

Survey your audience and ask for feedback using a Poll or Question sticker that not only allows them to participate but also allows you to create user generated content (the results or answers) that you can post to a future Story. Use these stickers to crowdsource ideas for content that your audience wants to consume.

The Poll sticker has become so popular, that Instagram now allows advertisers to create Instagram Story Ads featuring a Poll sticker which I can only assume means that they believe in its engagement effectiveness.

Engagement Stickers include: Poll, Question, Slider Scale, Quiz, Chat and Countdown

(*not all of the below options available on Facebook Stories currently)

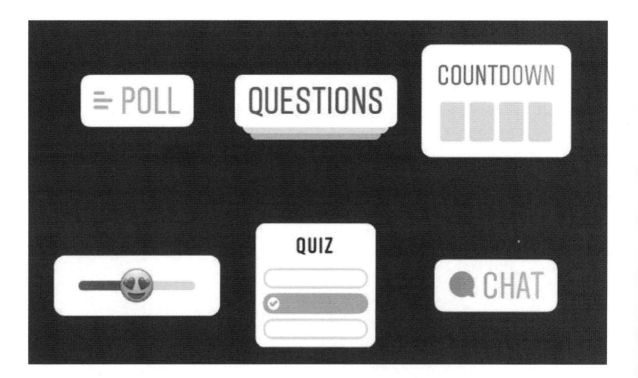

F - FORMATTING

Formatting matters!

If you want people to engage with your content, it needs to be in a format that's easy to consume and optimized for the algorithm.

• Format for "The Social Skim"

There's a behavioral model called Optimal Foraging Theory that explains why your posts aren't getting the engagement they deserve! In short, this theory says our brains burn a ton of calories making decisions and processing data every second of the day, so to save it from getting burnt out, we only process the most important data.

Here's a modern day example:

↳ You attend a real estate conference in a huge hotel ballroom. When you walk into the room, you likely aren't counting the number of seats in the room, but you do know where the exits are in case of an emergency.

That's Optimal Foraging Theory – your brain is taking in the important stuff and skipping over the data that makes our brains burn calories!

What does this have to do with your posts?

Tech, screens and endless Feeds have changed the way our brains process information, especially the way we read. When you post a piece of content that has a lot of text (and small font on top of that) like a newsletter our brains say, "Nope, that's way too many calories for me to burn" and we keep on scrolling. This is why Instagram was such a hit – easy for our brains to process pictures.

Increase your engagement by formatting your posts for what I call the "Social Skim." Short, one- sentence paragraphs with spacing because our brains want bullet points, not one giant blob of words. You can easily create bullets or visual separation by using emoji or even punctuation marks in between your one sentence paragraphs in captions.

** **NOTE:** Instagram isn't as formatting friendly as other platforms. If you've ever tried to craft a caption that converts including eye-pleasing spacing between your short paragraphs only to post it and see that your sentences have been smooshed into one giant lump, then you know this pain all too well.

Here's a few tips to keep your Insta content in the Social Skim format:

↳ Use the free website **Apps4LifeHost.com** to keep the spacing and formatting for your captions. Simply paste the caption text into the content box, click the Convert button and your formatting is saved and ready to be pasted into the Instagram caption box.

↳ Use a paid third party platform scheduler like Later.com to maintain spacing or try out the new free Creator Studio website for Instagram (although it's a bit buggy sometimes).

↳ Use punctuation or emoji to separate your paragraphs like this:

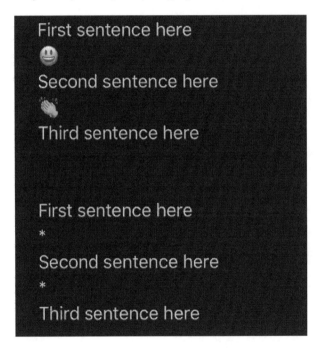

• Leverage the **[...see more]** auto formatting for your posts

Don't be afraid to write mini blog posts in your captions! There's no rule for caption length but you do want to make sure you're structuring your captions as described in Chapter 8.

When more than a sentence or two is typed into your caption box, The Socials will automatically truncate or abbreviate the body of your text by adding the [...see more] to your post. The reason for this is to maximize the visuals in your post not the text as our brains process visuals faster and more often than words.

Include a visual call to action such as the hand pointing down emoji to indicate to readers that there's more down below!

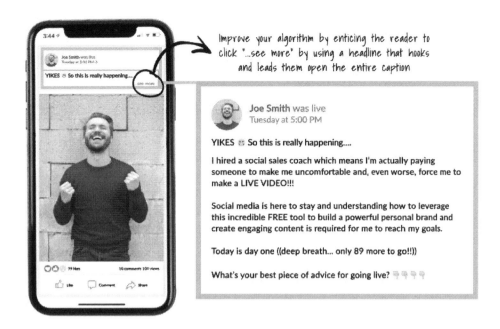

Improve your algorithm by enticing the reader to click "...see more" by using a headline that hooks and leads them open the entire caption

Joe Smith was live
Tuesday at 5:00 PM

YIKES 😬 So this is really happening....

I hired a social sales coach which means I'm actually paying someone to make me uncomfortable and, even worse, force me to make a LIVE VIDEO!!!

Social media is here to stay and understanding how to leverage this incredible FREE tool to build a powerful personal brand and create engaging content is required for me to reach my goals.

Today is day one ((deep breath... only 89 more to go!!))

What's your best piece of advice for going live? 👇👇👇👇

- Add text to your Facebook and Instagram Stories

While Stories are watched more with the sound on than without, adding some context to your content is helpful to those watching silently because our brains can't help but read when it sees words. Formatting your Story content with text can grab a Story viewer's attention and potentially increase engagement.

Imagine creating a short Story video talking about the new Netflix series you watched over the weekend. In your video and you ask if anyone has watched it and you also add text to your video that says: "have you seen [Series Name] on Netflix yet?"

Now those viewers watching without sound can understand what you're talking about AND may send you a direct message that they wouldn't have been able to send without hearing your question. It can also encourage a viewer to stop tapping and turn on the sound if your text sparks their interest.

It's not necessary to type out verbatim what you are saying in the video but providing some anchor points of reference will increase your engagement.

PRO TIP

Don't force people to consume your content the way you think it should be consumed! Just because you made a video doesn't mean everyone wants to watch it – some would prefer to read that same content. Adding a text description, summary or important bullet points to any video post in Facebook or LinkedIn is helpful to those viewers who may not want to watch your video. I recommend adding a summary of what you're talking about in written form as well so people can still consume and engage with your content.

G - GROUPS

• Facebook Groups

Facebook has stated that Groups are a major focus for their algorithm moving forward because they encourage meaningful conversations amongst users. Depending on the Group rules, you can share your content in the Group as long as it's helpful, educational and appropriate.

Your content will be seen by all members which can help you build brand. Actively participating and answering other Group members' questions will increase your credibility.

You can also create your own private or paid Group which allows you to create original content that your members are more likely to see (over Page posts), host Watch Parties, Live Video trainings and create learning modules called Units. As the Group founder and admin, you are viewed as a leader and a connector.

• Engagement Groups (Pods)

An engagement group (more commonly referred to as a 'Pod') is a group of people who have agreed to like, comment and share each other's content on a specified platform within minutes of it being posted.

Getting comments within the first few minutes of posting triggers more reach and therefore more engagement which is why almost all Pods maintain rules about designated commenting times for all members.

These groups are not against the platforms Terms of Service at this time; however, being an active Pod member does require a level of commitment to engage with multiple people's content which can feel like a lot of work.

H - HASHTAGS

Using relevant, well-researched hashtags helps your content get discovered by people who search for a specific topic/keyword.

A hashtag works like the old school card catalog at the library. Each card has a number on it that corresponds to the location that a book is stored on a specific shelf. Hashtags are like that card that helps you find the book, except in this case they help you find topics, accounts and content within social media platforms not physical objects.

Hashtags allow your content to become searchable by keyword(s). By using the hashtag **#sandiegohomes** on your post related to homes for sale in San Diego, a consumer can now find your post by searching that hashtag. Instagram even tracks the number of people who have seen your posts as a direct result of a hashtag search (check Post Insights).

Three major Instagram hashtag mistakes:

Hashtags are typically used within Instagram, Twitter and LinkedIn. While you can use them on Facebook, it's not the "language" of that platform (which is why it's not always ideal to automatically cross-post from Instagram to Facebook).

1. Not using enough per post (Yes, you really do need to use 15-20+ per post!)

2. Using popular or "big" hashtags. **#realestate** has been used in over 30 million posts! Your post will not likely rank for such a popular hashtag because so many other accounts are using it. It's also important to mix or 'layer' your hashtag sizes! Layering your hashtags means using some semi-popular hashtags and some less popular more niche hashtags. The more popular hashtags can help you get some initial reach and engagement while the smaller ones will attract your ideal audience and offer more longevity for your post.

2. Using NON relevant hashtags. Your ideal customer is likely not looking for **#topproducer** but they could be looking for home related topics, décor or design hashtags and most importantly, location specific keywords. It's important that you spend time researching what hashtags your ideal customer is searching for and not that describe your industry. **#realtor** tells us what you do, but are consumers really searching that word in Instagram?

**If you want to master Instagram strategy, I highly recommend following Jenn Herman @ jenns_trends, subscribing to her YouTube channel, her blog Jennstrends.com and purchasing her books – she's my personal mentor who has taught me and tens of thousands of others about how to use Instagram the right way!

I - INSIGHTS

The very best way to increase post engagement is to make content that fulfills your specific community's desires. In other words, give 'em what they want. The number of comments and shares your content receives helps you understand what your audience craves. Diving deeper into the analytics of your post will help you deliver the kind of content your community wants.

The only surefire way to know what your audience wants is to review your insights and performance analytics. Establishing a baseline for your content performance can help you identify what formats and topics of content generates more conversations and conversions.

You might be surprised to learn that the posts you predicted would perform well didn't. You might discover that one type of content is outperforming others and by creating similar content in the future, you will ensure higher levels of post engagement. If quote posts get more shares, then do more of those. If photos of your face always get more comments, do more of that! If posts about your listings get the least amount of engagement, then your strategy needs to change.

The content evolution should look something like this:

Observe > support other's content > start making your own content > review metrics to improve content

Don't get overly analytical! Measuring is meant to help you but shouldn't become an overbearing task that makes you overthink what to post or prevent you from having fun with social media!

**NOTE: Insights are available for Facebook Business Pages, Instagram Business and Instagram Creator accounts.

(See the next chapter on metrics)

J – JARGON-FREE

The average consumer isn't familiar with your industry specific jargon. It's like watching Gray's Anatomy and hoping to understand all of the medical terminology used in each episode. Using lingo that is commonly used by someone in your field in your content or advertising is doing your content a disservice. In fact, it confuses people and makes them feel excluded or even embarrassed that they aren't "in the know."

Here's an example of jargon:

> **"Conforming loan limits just increased – Hooray!"**

The consumer is wondering: "what the heck is a conforming loan limit and why should I be happy about it?"

Do you think they will leave a comment asking what a conforming loan limit is – no! They assume that everyone else must know what it is and don't want to feel embarrassed by asking.

So, they keep on scrolling.

How about this one:

> **"Don't get stuck with a Cloud on Title"**

Do you think the average consumer has any idea what a Cloud is other than where their photos are stored? Why should they care?

One more:

> **"I provide extraordinary service for all your real estate needs from start to finish"**

FLUFF is also JARGON.

I expect extraordinary service.

You should fulfill all my real estate needs, you're a real estate agent and that's your job.

Yes, it would be ideal if we started the process together and you finished it.

Keep your content simple, straight to the point and easy to understand to generate more conversations. Explaining concepts isn't dumbing it down, it's showing your audience that you really understand what you do and WHY it matters to them.

Make the hard to understand stuff easy. (That could be your superpower!)

K - KEYWORDS EVERYWHERE

This is a chrome plug-in that pulls the "People Also Search For" and "Related" keywords from Google and shows them to you with the volume metrics right inside Google's search page.

Knowing what people are searching for can help your engagement because you know exactly what to post that people want to see – it also will give you the right keywords to use in your blog post and YouTube titles for better discoverability and ranking – higher ranking = more views = more engagement.

L – LEAVE IT FOR LATER

Creating content shouldn't feel like a chore or create more stress in your life. One of the ways to decrease your content anxiety is to save it for later – meaning, get prepared for those content days when you're feeling uninspired!

Write down ideas throughout the week on a notepad, bookmark articles for later and take photos often and simply don't post them in the moment!

I take photos all of the time and they sit in my camera roll for days, weeks and months. I may post some of the photos from my vacation, but I also keep one or two that could be used in a future post. A lot of folks call it "Latergramming" instead of "Insta(nt)gramming" and it's a super simple and effective way to create more content with much less stress!

M – "MAGIC IN THE MUNDANE"

This is another Chelsea-ism that means it's ok to post about your everyday 'boring' life.

At the end of the day, we sit around our dining tables or couches with friends and family and talk about mundane topics. Those are the conversations that humanize us and make us feel connected. Why do you think millions of people like to watch celebrity behind the scenes content? Because they're doing normal, everyday things just like you.

Every piece of content you make won't be a home run and won't appeal to everyone, even in your niche audience but ANY topic can be made into engaging content!!!

I once created a Story at Costco asking viewers if they were "team cube" or "team rectangle" when it came to Kleenex box preference. 351 comments later, team cube won by a mile. I post about the school pick up line shenanigans and the weird plant that won't stop growing in my front yard. I have FUN with those relatable human stories and invite people to engage with them.

Try this: think about parts of your larger story and extract little nuggets. Instead of posting about going to Costco, can you post about your favorite item to purchase there and ask others if they buy it? What about the samples on Sunday – can you create a funny sequence of Stories rating each sample? What was the worst sample of the day?

I get it – you don't like seeing people's salad posts in the Feed and why would anyone care about your day to day? Quality is Subjective, but that goes both ways. You may think your content is boring but someone else who really needs to learn about the escrow process and found your educational video on YouTube is exactly what they needed. They had a need and your "boring" content fulfilled it. Allow your audience to determine if content is valuable in a specific context.

I'm not suggesting that if you only post a photo of your coffee mug every day that you're going to generate engagement or build a community. What I am saying is I don't want you to not post or overthink your content because you're afraid that it's not exciting enough.

Don't let your fear hold you back – how will you know what works if you don't test it out?

N – NATIVE CONTENT

The Socials prefer natively uploaded content (especially Facebook!) This means if you have a great YouTube video, it won't get as much reach or engagement if you share it from YouTube to Facebook. Instead, directly upload the YouTube video into Facebook as an original post.

O - OPTIMIZE ORGANIC CONTENT WITH PAID ADS

This workbook is about creating organic or FREE content but that doesn't mean you shouldn't consider optimizing content that's already gotten some organic love – comments, shares etc. Social media ads (Facebook & Instagram Ads, Linkedin Ads and YouTube Pre-Roll ads) can be extremely effective for building brand awareness, driving traffic to a lead capture landing page and generating LEADS in a cost effective way.

The most commonly used platform to create social media ad campaigns is Facebook Ads Manager which is built into Facebook.com. It's a robust platform that allows you to target people using location and online behaviors. You're able to upload customer lists and create additional 'custom audiences' to which you can then serve ads.

Examples of Custom Audiences:

- People in your database (can upload a .csv file into system)
- People who've engaged at all with your Facebook Business Page or Instagram Business Account (like post, saved post, direct message etc)
- People who've sent you a DM
- People who've visited your website
- People who've watched your videos
  And more....

You can also 'retarget' people with future ads who have engaged with your content or visited your website. Re-targeting is what happens when you click through Amazon and find something you may want to buy but then decide not to complete the purchase and the next thing you know that item is 'following' you around the internet and ads are showing up in your social Feed!

We could write an entire book just on ads, so I'll keep it short and sweet:

- Ads can generate leads, but you still need to convert them
- Create a budget and maintain a long term mindset
- Set up a CRM and email nurture campaign
- Paid campaigns actually are more effective with a solid organic content foundation. If I click on your ad, I want to stalk your organic content like your Stories and your YouTube videos too!

P – PROACTIVE PARTICIPATION

If you want more engagement, you need to initiate it!

So many people tell me, "I'm posting consistently, but I hardly ever get any comments."

To which I reply, "Are you commenting on other's posts? Are you watching their Stories and sending them DMs?"

By supporting other people's content, you most certainly will increase the engagement on your own posts. This is the exactly how to become a Superfan and train your algorithm at the same time.

Here's a few actionable tactics to help you stay efficient and strategic when it comes to actively engaging on The Socials:

• **Create Facebook Friends Lists:**

Facebook allows users to add friends to lists without them knowing they've been added to a list. Creating these lists allows you to be efficient and strategic in your commenting because Selecting any **friend list** will clear out your homepage Feed and only show you a new custom news feed of posts made by just those **friends**. You'll never miss their posts again!

** Friends lists are not accessible via mobile app and they may at some point be removed altogether. How to make a list:

1. Access Facebook.com > Look at the left hand nagivation options > Look under "Explore" section for "Friends Lists" > Click on Friends List

2. Click Create List > Name list > Add friends to list by name

• Turn on Instagram Post Notifications:

You can enable push notifications for any Instagram account you follow to ensure that you never miss their posts. When that account makes a new post, you will receive a notification. You can then be one of the first people to comment and support their content. This strategy can also help you gain more followers by commenting on larger 'influencer' accounts. Typically, as the first commenter, your username will be seen by all others who comment and may pique curiosity and drive profile visits and follows.

1. Must be following the account to turn on notifications > Access Profile > Tap "Following" button > Tap on Notifications and make selection(s)

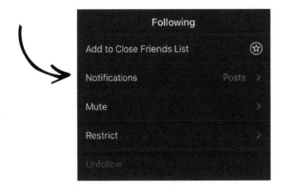

• Use Facebook's "See First" option:

When you select a person or Page to **see first**, their posts appear at the top of News Feed each time you open your app. The person or Page won't know you selected them to see first. Unfortunately, you're limited to a max of 30 'see firsts'.

1. Log into Facebook.com > Click on menu dropdown arrow top right > Scroll down to News   Feed preferences > Click Prioritize who to **see first**.

Q - Q & A

There are over 3.5 billion Google searches every SECOND of every day. Your customers are looking for answers and their questions will create highly engaging ideas for your content. Create content that answers your customers' most asked questions and crowdsource content ideas by adding polls and question stickers on your Stories.

Guess what my audience's most asked question is?

R – REPLY/QUESTION LOOP

This is a simple yet extremely effective engagement boosting strategy! Remember, the algorithms are looking for a 'relationship' between two people and 'meaningful interactions'.

Each time you receive a comment on your post, it triggers the algorithm to show that post to more people. When you reply to those comments, it shows the algorithm that you are a good community member and creating conversations. If those replies receive more replies back, the algorithm continues to re-bump that post out to more people.

You can strategically increase your engagement and reach by implementing the Reply/Question Loop:

> Every time you receive a comment on ANY platform, 'like' or 'love' that comment, reply to it and **then ask a question.**

> When you ask a question, it sends a notification to the commenter and they almost always reply back = algorithm trigger!

Here's an example:

> You make a post asking for recommendations to the best pizza place in your city. Someone comments with a location. You like the comment, reply "thanks" and ask this question: "do they have happy hour there too?"

Another example:

> Comment: "Thanks for the great video!"
> Reply: "My pleasure [@name]! Have you been there yet?"

BONUS TIPS:

- Re-bump your 'greatest hits': You can also revitalize older posts by commenting on them.

  For example: You posted the question about the best pizza place and received multiple comments. Two weeks later, you visited one of those pizza places and you reply to the person who suggested it with a thank you and photo of yourself there. That post will now re-circulate for a bit!

- Delayed Comments: While the algorithms are watching to see how much activity your posts receive in the first 30-60 minutes, you can also stretch the life of your posts by strategically delaying some of your replies.

  For Example: Your pizza post is receiving quite a few comments. You reply to half of them using the Reply/Question Loop and then come back in a few hours or even later that same day to reply to the remaining comments – each time it re-bumps the algorithm. I've personally experienced stretching the life of a post from 1 day to 3-4 days with this strategy.

** DON'T leave your commenters hanging though! If you only have one or two comments, you should reply to them quickly!

Stories Feed

S - STORIES

Facebook and Instagram offer a newer posting format called Stories. Essentially, there are now two separate Feeds - one across the top for Stories and then the main Feed that we are used to scrolling through that appears below it.

Photo credit: https://about.instagram.com/blog/announcements/introducing-instagram-stories

A Story is a photo or a short video clip that will disappear from your Story feed after a 24 hour period. Think of a Story as a collection of short visual pieces of your day that are strung together to showcase a 24 hour period of your life. Disappearing content is about being in real time and also about attention. When people miss your Story, they don't get a replay!

Attention is shifting towards the Story format because they promote real time engagement in a private one to one environment. There are no public vanity metrics (likes) and all comments are sent through direct message.

Stories are a highly engaging visual content format designed to increase interaction because they offer:

Camera First communication
Real time engagement
Message enabled private conversations

Over the last few years, the Story format has surpassed any photo or video content posted in the Feeds. They've become so popular that over 280,000 Instagram Stories are created every minute of every day as compared to 55,000 photo posts in the Feed (source: domo.com)

Earlier this year, Facebook founder Mark Zuckerberg made this statement about the future of Stories:

"We expect Stories are on track to overtake posts and feeds as the most common way that people share across all social apps. That's because Stories is a better format for sharing multiple video clips throughout your day. The growth of Stories will have an impact on how we build product and think about our business, including WhatsApp and Instagram, which are the No. 1 and No. 2 most-used Stories products in the world."

The ability to talk to someone in real time on a live video or by commenting on their Instagram or Facebook Story accelerates trust and creates a feeling of intimacy, or that "I feel like I already know you" experience. Turns out, there's a legitimate and proven science behind social media and how we connect as humans. Our brains don't know the difference between seeing someone's face on a device or seeing it in the same room.

I wrote my first book on this very topic - how cameras and real time social video changed the way we build trust through technology.

Here's a visual summary of my first book: *Talking in Pictures: How Snapchat Changed Cameras, Communication and Communities:*

There is a science to screen to screen communication. Our brains see your face and begin to know, like and trust you. Through sharing your story in real time, your audience becomes a part of your story and we build community through shared experiences. Lastly, as we invest time into building our online communities, we become committed to continuing that process.

📷 CAMERA FIRST FORMULA

SCIENCE:
FACES ACCELERATE **TRUST**

SOCIOLOGY:
REAL TIME SHARED EXPERIENCES CREATE **COMMUNITY**

PSYCHOLOGY:
INVESTMENT IS **COMMITMENT**

The camera is the new feed which means that today's consumer expects to see your face and engage with your brand in real time - industry is irrelevant but behavior is not.

THE ▷ IS THE NEW SOCIAL FEED

We now build trust through technology:

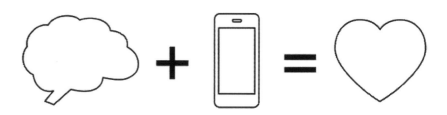

Ultimately, the Story format is an excellent way to increase your engagement because Stories offer private one to one messaging and is the ONLY social content format that allows you to see who's watching!! If I broadcast a Facebook live, the only people I know for certain saw my video are those who commented or liked the post. It allows you to be authentic and relatable and build trust by showing your face. Leverage this content format to showcase the behind the scenes of your day to day and the more personal side of your content.

T - TAGGING

Tagging other accounts that are relevant to your post's topic, as a shout out to an account or to identify who appears in a photo is a surefire way to get a more love on your posts. You should never abuse tagging as it's poor social media etiquette and likely to get you 'action blocked' by The Socials.

Over-tagging accounts can trigger bot software on some platforms and land you in 'jail' for a period of time which prevents you from taking certain actions on that platform such as posting, commenting or tagging. It's also really annoying to most people to be tagged with everyone under the sun in an attempt to get more reach.

U - UPLIFT YOUR COMMUNITY

Become a Superfan.

A Superfan is someone who supports other's content, builds their brand awareness by commenting and also demonstrates to the algorithms that they are a 'good community member' who engages in meaningful conversations.

Here's a few tips to grow your community on your way to Superfandom:

- Watch who views your Stories and send them a DM voice message thank you (and watch their stories!)

- Send a video message asking how YOU can help someone build their business or ask what their biggest need is for the week (you may not be able to fulfill it but the ask is important)

- Every time you make a new connection or receive a new follow send them a DM – bonus points if it's a voice message

- Be a connector!!! Make introductions via DMs to people that can mutually benefit from connecting

- Offer something for free with no strings attached, no email requirement and no follow up with a sales pitch or ask of any kind

- Shout outs! Share other people's posts and accounts and let your community know WHY they should follow that account as well!

As you become someone's Superfan, you're consistently building goodwill, brand and trust and all of those things will increase your overall engagement and reach.

V - VANITY METRICS

These are metrics that you CAN measure but that don't impact your bottom line.

Likes, View Counts and Followers are considered vanity metrics. Sure, these metrics can give you an indication of if your content is engagement worthy, but they don't directly lead to sales. The problem with these kinds of metrics is that they can be easily manipulated (paying for likes or followers) and don't correlate to tangible indicators of business success.

Likes: Instagram recently announced testing the removal of all public likes on posts in an attempt to reduce stress. This only supports the idea that likes shouldn't be the primary performance metric.

Views: Views are hard to accurately measure at this time. Bots (automated software) are rampant and driving up inauthentic view counts. Don't get caught up in the total number of views; instead, focus on watch time and comments. If 'only' 10 people watch your Instagram Story, that's 10 people who chose to spend some of their time engaging with your content (and hopefully your face!)

Followers: Community growth does matter. The more people you can share your message with the more opportunity for additional business. However, your goal should be to connect with IDEAL community members not every person online. Going deeper with your current community should be the first step before you attempt to go wider with a new audience. Create raving fans by becoming their superfan. Be consistently supporting others content and thoughtfully crafting your own.

What really matters is the number of conversations you are having on a daily basis, referrals you receive and conversions that take place.

W - WHEN TO POST

One way to get more comments is posting when your audience is active on the platform. There's no magic posting time that works for everyone. Knowing when your audience is online is important to your algorithm because the more comments you get, the more reach you receive. If you're posting at midnight and most of your community is already asleep, that may not be the best strategy.

Generally speaking, we're checking our phones in the morning, at lunchtime and before bed. Typically, morning to mid-afternoon times garner higher levels of engagement as do mid-week days. The best way to determine when your audience is online is to check your in-app Insights.

PRO TIP

Check out the "When to Post" app for the best times to post on Instagram (IOS only)

X - X-MARKET YOUR CONTENT

(There are hardly any words that start with X that I can pronounce, so I did my best here!)

If you want more reach, you must share your content with the world in as many ways as possible! Tell people where to follow you and find your content. You need to market your marketing! Increase your brand exposure and connect more people to your content by marketing it across multiple platforms and combining digital and traditional marketing methods.

- Cross-promote your handles for all platforms on all of your About You pages
- Include social handles, links and URLS on your Facebook, YouTube and LinkedIn Cover photos
- Add YouTube and Instagram tabs to your Facebook Business Page
- Use a branded hashtag at a live event, contest and on printed marketing materials
- Add handles to your Email signatures (check out WiseStamp.com) and business cards
- Include media files on your LinkedIn Profile to direct visitors to a variety of web links

Y - YOURSELF

As in, do it yourself.

Social Media is about YOU being social with other people- not your assistant, not your marketing agency, not your third party software. While each of those resources can improve your efficiency and streamline content related tasks, it's critical to allow consumers to experience your brand firsthand. Our behaviors have become trained to expect to see the person behind the brand and be able to connect with them through a direct message.

Huge brands like Nike pay celebrities millions of dollars to use their faces because they understand the power of human connection. You have a distinct advantage over these big brands because you can easily share your face and your story with the click of a button.

Whether you agree with it or not, many consumers will pick their next Realtor® based on the number of YouTube videos they've posted or how many star ratings appear on their Facebook Page. The ability to watch someone's daily Story could be the determining factor for someone to send an email requesting a meeting.

The best part of sharing your own story is that your content does the 'selling' for you. By the time you meet with a potential client across the table, they already feel like they know you from watching your videos, seeing your photos and listening to your voice. You've built instant rapport and credibility through your content.

Learning how to do something firsthand like editing a video or creating a social media graphic can teach you new skills that can be applied elsewhere in your business. Getting comfortable on live video will certainly improve your public speaking and in-person presentations. This doesn't mean that you have to do these things forever, but the learning process often teaches you something invaluable and gives you some 'street cred.'

Z - ZERO EXCUSES

You've read this book.

You know the why, the what and the how.

Now, do the work.

ENSURE YOUR EFFECTIVENESS

"A useful metric is both accurate (in that it measures what it says it measures) and aligned with your goals. Don't measure anything unless the data helps you make a better decision or change your actions."

Seth Godin, Author

MEASURING YOUR CONTENT'S EFFECTIVENESS

If you're creating content, you should be measuring it.

The act of creating and publishing content is only the first step to building your brand and business. Getting your ideal customer to engage with your content and take action is what generates more income for your family.

You can't create conversions if your content misses the mark with your audience.

Reviewing your content analytics helps you understand what's working and what isn't. Luckily, The Socials offer in-app insights that can help track your content's performance and optimize the success of your future posts.

*Note: In some cases, you may only be able to access detailed analytics for specific platforms or goals with paid third-party systems.

Here's a brief overview of *some* of the metrics you can review to evaluate the success of your content:

- **Brand Awareness:** *Reach, Impressions, @ Mentions/Tags, Follower Growth, Subscriptions*
- **Engagement:** *Likes, Comments, Shares, Bookmarks, Engagement Rate, Story & Video Views, Watch time, Downloads, Direct Messages, Screenshots*
- **Traffic:** *Profile visits, Website visits, Link Clicks, Swipe Ups*
- **Leads:** *Lead form submissions*
- **Conversions:** *Closed transactions sourced from social media*

UNDERSTANDING YOUR FACEBOOK INSIGHTS

Your Facebook Business Page is the only part of Facebook that shows your content insights and analytics. Your Personal Profile does not offer metric measurement reports but you can still track some of these manually (# of comments, likes etc)

There are two ways you can view your Facebook Page content insights:

1. On the "Insights" tab of your Facebook Business Page
2. Via the Facebook Creator Studio website business.facebook.com/creatorstudio

FACEBOOK BUSINESS PAGE INSIGHTS TAB

- Navigate to your Facebook Business Page
- Tap on Insights
- Select an option from the left hand navigation menu
- The "Overview" Tab will display all metrics on one page while you can easily "deep dive" into more details by clicking on the individual metric options below

FACEBOOK CREATOR STUDIO

The Creator Studio is a newer website created by Facebook to bring together all the tools you need to effectively post, manage, monetize and measure content across all your Facebook Pages and Instagram accounts. Most of the data contained within your Insights Tab on Your Business Page can also be found in this website's dashboard.

Creator Studio tracks the performance of your videos (the videos you share and the videos you crosspost) across all your Facebook Pages. Additionally, this site will track information about your audience, how often they're watching and when people are returning to watch most often ("loyalty" metrics) and overall account growth.

Video Performance Metrics:

The insights at the top of the **Performance** section in Creator Studio don't show insights into specific videos. Instead, insights are aggregated based on the Page or Pages you select at the top of your screen.

To see performance insights for specific videos, scroll down the Page to the **Top Videos** tab.

Here, you can see a list of your top videos, along with the Page that posted it and these options:

- **1-Minute Video Views:** The number of times your videos were played for at least 1 minute. During a single instance of a video playing, we'll count video views separately and exclude any time spent replaying the video.

- **Minutes Viewed:** The total number of minutes your videos were played including time spent replaying the video.

- **3-Second Video Views:** The number of times your videos were played for at least 3 seconds, or for nearly their total length if they're shorter than 3 seconds, within the selected time range. During a single instance of a video playing, we'll exclude any time spent replaying the video.

- **Engagement:** The number of people who reacted, commented or shared one of your videos.

- **Net Followers:** The number of new followers minus the number of unfollows during the defined period of time. Any new followers who have joined multiple Pages in your collection will only be counted once per period.

** You can also break down your metrics to understand what proportion is organic vs. paid.

https://www.facebook.com/business/help/214952509306377?id=203539221057259

LOYALTY INSIGHTS

The **Loyalty** tab in Creator Studio's Facebook section includes insights on:

- **Follower Activity:** See how many people followed or unfollowed you over the selected period of time. Net followers are the number of new followers minus the number of people who unfollowed during this period. Any new followers who have joined multiple Pages in your collection will only be counted once per period.

- **Returning Viewers:** Track the loyalty of your audience with a week-by-week look at returning viewers. A returning viewer is someone who viewed at least 1 minute of one of your videos in the previous week and returned to view at least 1 minute of one of your videos the following week.

- **How Long People Are Watching:** Get the number of 3-Second Views (the number of times your video played for at least 3 seconds, or for nearly its total length if it's shorter than 3 seconds), 15-Second Views (the number of times your video played for 15 seconds, or for 97% of its total length if it's shorter than 15 seconds) and 1-Minute Views (the number of times your video played for at least 1 minute).

** Metrics are estimates. During a single instance of a video playing, Facebook counts video views separately and exclude any time spent replaying the video.

https://www.facebook.com/business/help/214952509306377?id=203539221057259

AUDIENCE INSIGHTS

Better understand who your audience is, where they live, what languages they speak and what interests they have.

The **Audience Insights** section shows you insights from the last 7 or 14 days on:

- **Engaged Viewers:** People who reacted to, commented on or shared one of your videos within the selected date range.

- **Viewers:** People who watched at least one minute of your videos within the selected date range.

- **New Followers:** People who have followed your Page or recently unfollowed it within the selected date range.

Whichever audience breakdown you select, you can see the following information about them:

- **Countries:** The top countries where your engaged viewers, viewers or new followers are located.

- **Language:** The top languages your engaged viewers, viewers or new followers prefer to use.

- **Interests:** Other interests your engaged viewers, viewers or new followers have.

- **Pages your audience likes:** Pages your engaged viewers, viewers, new followers and recent unfollowers also like or follow.

- **Videos your audience is watching:** Videos on Facebook that your engaged viewers, viewers or new followers are watching.

When viewing the **New Followers** audience breakdown, you can also see the hour, day or a combination of both which reflects when your followers use Facebook on any device over the past week. This insight is not available for the **Engaged Viewers** or **Viewers** audience breakdowns.

** All times are recorded in Pacific Time. Some of this data maybe delayed depending on your time zone and the time of day. All metrics are estimates and in development.

https://www.facebook.com/business/help/214952509306377?id=203539221057259

Stop Complicating Content - *Let's make this easy and straight to the point*

EARNINGS INSIGHTS

Earnings insights are insights from your videos with in-stream ads and come from the videos you uploaded, including any crossposts and shares of them. You won't see insights from your crossposts and shares of other people's videos.

Your insights are broken down into:

- **Estimated earnings:** This is an estimate of the amount you earned from ads in your videos, based on the number of impressions and CPM of ads shown. Final payments may differ from this estimate pending reviews, content ownership claims and other adjustments.

- **1-minute video views:** This number includes all views of 1 minute or longer for all your videos containing in-stream ads. Views of videos without ads are not included. 1-minute video views are important for monetization because an ad can be shown only after a viewer has watched a video for at least 1 minute. In-stream ad placement can vary from video to video and viewer to viewer, so this metric does not directly predict the number of ad impressions in your videos.

- **Monetizable View RPM:** This is the money you earn for every 1,000 1-minute or longer views of your videos with in-stream ads. An increase in your monetizable view RPM indicates that you're making more money from the same amount of views.

- **Ad CPM:** This is the amount of money advertisers paid to show 1,000 ad impressions in your content. Ad CPM is affected by many factors, including the time of year, the demographics of your audience, and the number of advertisers who want to reach your viewers. Remember, CPM reflects what advertisers are willing to pay, not what you will actually earn.

https://www.facebook.com/business/help/214952509306377?id=203539221057259

UNDERSTANDING INSTAGRAM INSIGHTS

If you have an Instagram Business or Creator Account, you can access native analytics that provide you with helpful data about your followers, their actions, account growth and the overall performance of your content.

*Note: Insights are NOT available for Personal accounts which means you will need to switch to a Business or Creator account in order to access them (Profile Menu > Settings > Account)

Instagram Insights saves data starting from the time you convert to a Business/Creator account. Any data prior to that date won't be saved.

THERE ARE THREE WAYS TO ACCESS INSIGHTS:

1. Via the Profile Menu Settings

2. Via Individual Posts or Stories

3. Via Creator Studio website

INSIGHTS FROM PROFILE MENU

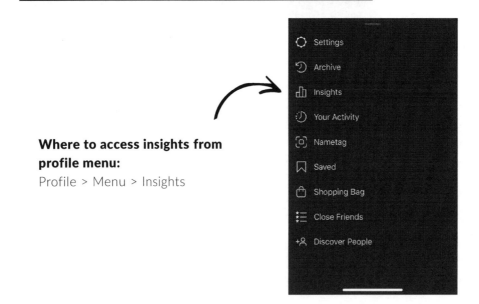

Where to access insights from profile menu:
Profile > Menu > Insights

After tapping on Insights, a new tab will appear showing Insights broken down into three categories: Content, Activity and Audience

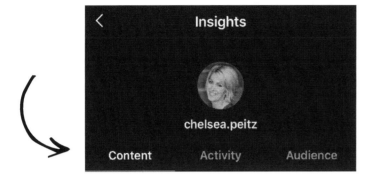

CONTENT INSIGHTS

This set of insights displays the combined number of Posts and Stories you created.

- **Posts:** The total number of posts created in the last 7 days, ordered by the number of times they were seen

- **Stories:** the total number of stories created in the last 24 hours ordered chronologically

Tapping on "See All" in the Posts section will bring you to another display page that will allow you to sort your content in a variety of ways which is very helpful to determine what kind of content is resonating with your audience:

FORMAT	TIME PERIOD	INTERACTIONS	
Photo posts	7 days	calls	likes
video posts	30 days	comments	profile visits
carousel posts	3 months	emails	reach
shopping posts	6 months	engagement	saved
	1 year	follows	shares
	2 years	get directions	texts
		impressions	website clicks

PRO TIPS

Sort by engagement, saved and shares to find your greatest hits and create similar content

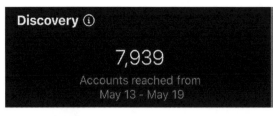

DISCOVERY is a set of insights that measures how many people see your content and where they find it.

- **Reach:** The number of unique accounts that have seen any of your posts. The reach metric is only an estimate

- **Impressions:** The total number of times all your posts have been seen

* Impressions typically will exceed Reach as one account could have viewed your post more than once. An easy way to remember: **Reach = # of people vs Impressions = # of views**

INTERACTIONS is a set of insights that measures the actions people take when they engage with your profile

- **Profile Visits:** The number of times your profile was viewed

- **Website Clicks:** The number of clicks on the link in your bio (this can be an indication that your Bio is lacking an enticing call to action!)

* Depending on what settings you've enabled in your account, additional interaction data will appear in this section such as: Get Directions, Calls, Call to Action Button Clicks

AUDIENCE INSIGHTS

This section displays demographic data about the people who follow you, their locations, days and times of follower activity and account growth

- **Growth:** You can track how your audience has grown in a single day or over 7 days.

- **Overall:** The number of accounts that followed you minus the number of accounts that unfollowed you

- **Followed You:** The number of accounts that followed you within your selected time frame

- **Unfollowed You:** The number of accounts that unfollowed you within your selected time frame

- **Top locations:** The top five cities and countries where your followers are located.

- **Age range:** Age range of followers

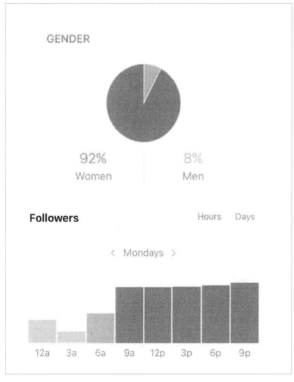

- **Gender:** Followers broken down by gender

- **Follower hours:** the average time of day your followers are on Instagram.

- **Follower days:** the days of the week your followers are most active.

INSIGHTS FROM A SINGLE FEED POST

You can also access insights for an individual Feed post directly from the post itself.

Find the post you want to review and tap on the blue words "View Insights" in the bottom right corner of the post:

- **Taps Forward:** The number of times a viewer tapped the right side of the screen to go to the next story. A lot of people "speed tap" through Stories, so paying attention to the Next Story swipes and Exits may offer more valuable information about your content.

- **Next Story:** The number of times viewers swiped to the next story after yours in the queue. If you see a high number here, it means people have lost interest and want to move on to the next story. Pay attention to this number!

- **Exits:** The number of times a viewer swipes down to stop watching stories and go back to the main feed. Exits tell you whether users watched your story to completion or if they exited before the story ended. Exits happen when:

  - Users swiped left (not tapped back or forward) to move to another user's story.
  - Users closed Instagram while viewing your story.

Once you tap on **View Insights**, a new menu appears that looks like this:

- **Hearts:** # of likes (public facing liked may be removed at some point)

- **Comments:** # of comments

- **Shares (Paper Airplane icon):** # of shares to Stories or via Direct Messages

- **Saves (Ribbon Icon):** Number of times someone saved or bookmarked your post

** Super important to the algorithm!
Saved content = valuable content (this is an excellent call to action to ask readers to bookmark your post!)

SWIPE UP on this section TO VIEW ADDITIONAL INSIGHTS

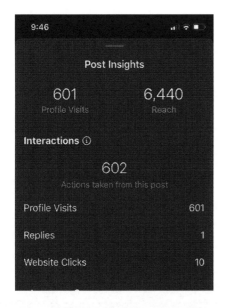

INTERACTIONS: This set of insights displays the number of actions taken on your account

- Profile visits generated from your post

- Total unique accounts your post reached

- Actions taken directly from your post: visiting your profile, a hyperlink, clicking the call/email button

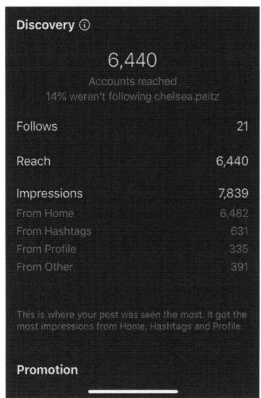

DISCOVERY: This set of insights measures how many people see your content and where they find it.

- **Reach:** The number of accounts reached through discovery who are not currently following you.

- **From Home:** From a user's home feed

- **From Hashtags:** From hashtags

- **From Location:** From location tag

- **From Other:**

  Impressions from **Other** could be generated by:
  - Posts that have been shared through direct messages
  - Posts that have been saved
  - Posts you've been tagged or mentioned in
  - Posts that show up on the **Following** tab in your notifications

STORY INSIGHTS

To access insights on your Story, tap on your active Story and swipe up to open a new page displaying data:

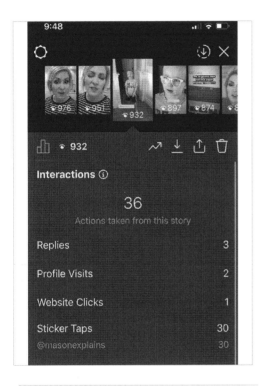

- **Eye Icon:** Number of Viewers and their names
- **Interactions:** shares, replies, profile visits, sticker taps (The number of times a viewer tapped on a location, hashtag or mention sticker in your Story)

- **Accounts Reached:** The number of unique accounts that viewed your story.

- **Impressions:** The number of times your story has been viewed.

NAVIGATION:

- **Taps Backward:** The number of times a viewer tapped the left side of the screen to rewatch the previous story. If someone is tapping back to rewatch something, that's a good thing! Can you identify what kind of content that was and create more like this?

- **Taps Forward:** The number of times a viewer tapped the right side of the screen to go to the next story. A lot of people "speed tap" through Stories, so paying attention to the Next Story swipes and Exits may offer more valuable information about your content.

- **Next Story:** The number of times viewers swiped to the next story after yours in the queue. If you see a high number here, it means people have lost interest and want to move on to the next story. Pay attention to this number!

- **Exits:** The number of times a viewer swipes down to stop watching stories and go back to the main feed. Exits tell you whether users watched your story to completion or if they exited before the story ended. Exits happen when:

  - Users swiped left (not tapped back or forward) to move to another user's story.
  - Users closed Instagram while viewing your story.
  - Users have clicked on the X on the top-right corner of your story.
  - Users have swiped down the media, thus going back to the main feed.

Exits carry slightly less negative meaning that a "Next Story" because there could be a lot of reasons someone may "exit" such as they swiped up and clicked a link from your Story or perhaps they just simply ran out of time to watch more Stories.

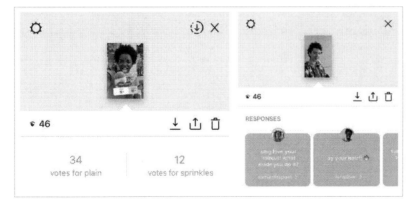

* Note: if you use engagement stickers on your Stories such as a poll or question sticker your results will also appear in this tab upon swipe up:

Image Credit: Later.com

** The last type of Story metric is "Mentions" which occur when someone mentions your account in their Story either by sharing your content to their Story or @ tagging your account. This metric sits at the top of your Notifications tab within the app and looks like this:

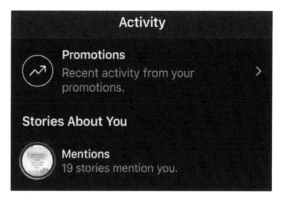

CREATOR STUDIO INSIGHTS

Instagram Creator Studio is a FREE online site created by Facebook/Instagram that allows you to manage and schedule posts and review paid and organic content insights. At this time, this desktop-only dashboard doesn't provide different analytics than the app itself does, it's anticipated that the site will evolve over time and introduce new tools that will allow users to further create, edit, manage, measure and monetize content across both Facebook and Instagram.

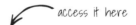

access it here

Business.facebook.com/creatorstudio

Once you've accessed Creator Studio, click on the Instagram logo at the top of the site and connect your account. Once connected, your insights dashboard will appear:

The content dashboard shows all of your photo, video, IGTV, Carousel and Stories post performance and You can also click any of the items in your list for more detailed data. You can also use the search bar to find and sort content.

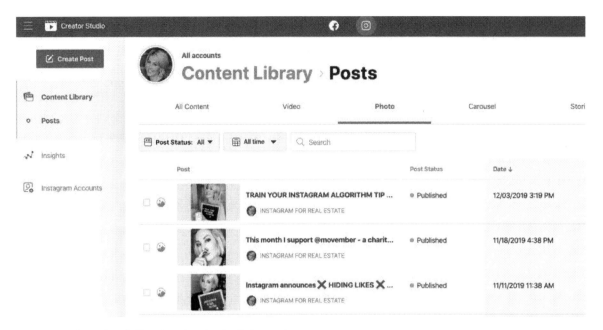

You can view the following in the **Insights** tab:

- **Audience:** information about your followers and audience, including their gender, age range and location.

- **Activity:** see what actions people take when they engage with your account. These can include profile or website visits, taps to call, text or email you, or taps to get directions to your business.

- **Accounts Reached:** Track the reach and total number of impressions of your content over the last 7 days.

100+ TOP TOOLS, TECH, APPS AND WEBSITES RESOURCE GUIDE

100+ TOP TOOLS, TECH, APPS AND WEBSITES RESOURCE GUIDE

Shout out to Easil.com who created the entire design for this workbook!

GRAPHIC DESIGN RESOURCES

EASIL.COM Your DIY secret weapon. Access 1000s of professionally designed, on-trend templates, including social media, Instagram Stories, infographics, posters, banners, menus and more. Design templates are all-inclusive. You pay nothing more to use included images
(FREE-$7.50/mo+)

CANVA.COM Drag-and-drop graphic design website & app. Some graphics are free
(FREE - $12.95/mo +)

GIPHY.COM MIllions of animated gifs for presentations, social media or blog posts. create and design your own and upload as well!
(FREE)

BEAUTIFUL.AI Create animated eye pleasing slide decks with their visual templates that adjust their design as you create them
(FREE- $12/mo+)

REMOVE.BG Remove the background from your images instantly!
(FREE)

DESIGNPICKLE.COM Unlimited custom graphic design and unlimited revisions done for you by your very own professional designer
(Pricing starting at $399/mo)

VISUAL.LY Eye-catching infographics for any of your presentation or social content needs
(Per project quote)

YOUTUBESCREENSHOT.COM
Grab screenshots from any YouTube video
(FREE)

BITEABLE.COM Make animated videos in seconds that you can use for Facebook Ads or social media posts
($20/mo+)

THENOUNPROJECT.COM
Icons for all your graphic design needs
(FREE)

PEXELS.COM Copyright free, high quality stock images & videos
(FREE)

VIDEO RESOURCES

JOBY GORILLAPOD TRIPOD

Flexible, universal smartphone and camera tripod
(Amazon $29+)

ARKON SPLEDRING CLIP ON SMARTPHONE RING LIGHT

Rechargeable, clip on smartphone light with three light level settings
(Arkon.com $15)

KIMAFUN LAV MIC SET

Wireless lapel mic system.
(Amazon $49+)

OSMO POCKET
The smallest 3-axis stabilized handheld camera
(Amazon $349+)

DJI OSMO SMARTPHONE GIMBAL

A lightweight video stabilizer
(Amazon $129+)

CANON POWERSHOT
G7X MARK II One of the most popular digital cameras used by YouTubers – this is NOT required, your iPhone camera is just as good, this is merely a suggestion should you want to invest in a traditional camera
(Amazon $649+)

NEEWER RING LIGHT

Dimmable LED standing ring light with multiple colored filter attachments, blue-tooth receiver and phone holder
(FREE - $8.25/mo+)

WAVE.VIDEO Upload your own videos or use included video clips to create and edit videos instantly
(FREE- $8.95/mo+)

REV.COM Outsource adding subtitles to any video
($1/min)

TEMI.COM Automate audio to text transcription
($0.10/min)

MAGISTO.COM An online video editing suite designed to simplify the video making process. The smart video maker presents the easiest way to transform videos and pictures into professionally crafted movies
(FREE - $5/mo+)

ANIMOTO.COM Combine your photos and video clips with music to make powerful, professional videos
(FREE - $5/mo+)

ADVANCED VIDEO EDITING SOFTWARE: iMovie, Screenflow, Camtasia, Adobe Premiere Pro
(Prices range)

LUMEN5.COM Transform articles into videos in minutes
(FREE - $19/mo+)

VIDIQ Analytics on YouTube video performance & keyword research
(FREE - $7.50/mo +)

TUBEBUDDY Analytics on YouTube video performance & keyword research
(FREE - $9/mo+)

VIDYARD GOVIDEO CHROME EXTENSION Record your webcam or capture your screen in just a few clicks. Share your video through Gmail and see who has viewed
(FREE)

VIDEO DOWNLOADER CHROME EXTENSION Download video from websites
(FREE)

CONTENT RESOURCES

TRELLO.COM /TRELLO APP
Organize content, plan projects and collaborate with others all in one place
(FREE - $9.99/mo+)

COSCHEDULE HEADLINE ANALYZER Helps you create better titles and headlines for YouTube videos and Blogs
(FREE)

ADVANCED MARKETING INSTITUTE HEADLINE Helps you create better titles and headlines for YouTube videos and Blogs
(FREE)

PORTENT'S CONTENT IDEA GENERATOR Instant blog topic inspiration
(FREE)

SIDEWAYSDICTIONARY.COM
Explains tech terms in the form of easy to understand analogies (ex: 2 Factor Authentication = Is like Cinderella's slipper)
(FREE)

FEEDLY.COM / FEEDLY APP
Organize, read and share the content of your favorite sites all in one place
(FREE - $5.41/mo+)

ANSWERTHEPUBLIC.COM A visual keyword research and content ideas tool *(FREE)*

KEYWORDS EVERYWHERE CHROME EXTENSION Chrome & Firefox add on that shows search volume, CPC & competition on websites *($2/mo)*

BREAKTHROUGHBROKER.COM Free online real estate marketing tools. Free marketing templates, instructional tools, current news and more. *(FREE)*

POSTPLANNER.COM Find engaging content ideas for your next social post *($3/mo+)*

42MATTERS.COM Access mobile app user data that you can upload into Facebook and serve ads to those people *($63/mo+)*

LIKEALYZER.COM Analyze any Facebook Business Page and get recommendations to optimize it *(FREE)*

FACEBOOK CREATIVE HUB Create mock ups for Facebook ads *facebook.com/ads/creativehub* *(FREE)*

BELIVE.TV Host dual or group Facebook Live broadcasts with customized logos *($20/mo+)*

MANYCHAT.COM Build your own Facebook Messenger chatbot without coding *(FREE- $10/mo+)*

CHATFUEL.COM Build your own Facebook Messenger chatbot without coding *(FREE- $15/mo+)*

FACEBOOK CREATOR STUDIO Facebook owned online dashboard that brings together all the tools you need to effectively post, manage monetize and measure content across all your Facebook Pages and Instagram accounts. It also helps you take advantage of new feature and monetization opportunities you may be eligible for *(FREE)* *business.facebook.com/creatorstudio*

"ELEVATED REAL ESTATE MASTERMIND" FACEBOOK GROUP
The best Facebook group for real estate related Facebook Ads training
(FREE)

ADCRATE.IO Curated top performing ad images, headlines, ad copy, targeting, and follow up scripts to make your real estate facebook marketing easier.
($99/mo)

LATER.COM – Visually plan, analyze & schedule Instagram posts
(FREE - $9/mo+)

PLANN APP Visually plan, analyze & schedule Instagram posts
(FREE - $6/mo+)

PLANOLY.COM / PLANOLY APP
Visually plan, analyze & schedule Instagram posts
(FREE - $7/mo+)

UNFOLD APP Create Instagram Stories with beautiful templated designs
(FREE - $2+)

LINKTREE.COM Add more links to your Instagram Bio
(FREE - $6/mo)

HASHTRACKING.COM Monitor and analyze social media campaigns via hashtags
($60/mo+)

HASTAGIFY.COM Find & analyze top hashtags in Twitter and Instagram
($19/mo+)

REPOST APP Repost Instagram posts with crediting original creator
(FREE - $5)

LINKINBIO (FROM LATER.COM)
Link individual Instagram posts to specific articles, websites, videos & more. Add multiple links to one Instagram post
(FREE - $9/mo+)

AGORAPULSE.COM
An easy to use social media management software that allows you to drive engagement and build authentic relationships with your audience all in one platform.
($79/mo+)

WHEN TO POST APP

The app generates a heat map with details on when during the day is best to post to Instagram, based on when the largest amount of your followers are browsing their Instagram feeds. You can see each day of the week, and get hour-by-hour analysis by tapping on a specific day.
(FREE- $1.99+)

INSTAGRAM CREATOR STUDIO

Instagram owned online dashboard that brings together all the tools you need to effectively post, manage, monetize and measure content across all your Facebook Pages and Instagram accounts. It also helps you take advantage of new features and monetization opportunities you may be eligible for.
(FREE)

business.instagram.com/creatorstudio

SOCIAL MEDIA APP RESOURCES

PHOTO EDITING

BEFUNKY Easy photo editing
(FREE)

VSCO What the "influencers" use to edit social photos
(FREE - $19+)

8MM Old fashioned photo/video effects
(FREE)

COLORSTORY Enhance your photo color effects
(FREE)

BACKGROUND ERASER
Erase parts of your images
(FREE)

SNAPSEED Photo Editor
(FREE)

RIPL Make videos from photos
(FREE - $15/mo+)

MEMATIC Make memes to share on social
(FREE- $4.99/mo+)

ADOBE LIGHTROOM
Basically, Photoshop on your phone
(this is my preferred tool!)
(FREE- $4.99/mo+)

TEXT OVERLAYS

HYPETYPE Animate your Text
(FREE - $1.99+)

ADOBE SPARK POST Templated designs for social posts
(FREE - $10/mo+)

APPLE CLIPS Add captions to your videos (iOS ONLY)
(FREE)

WORDSWAG Add fonts to your photos
(FREE - $5)

LEGEND Thumb-stopping animated posts (iOS ONLY)
(FREE)

VIDEO APPS

INSHOT Edit video, add text, add emojis, change background colors
(FREE)

VIDEOSHOP Edit video, slow motion, add music, voice overs
(FREE)

VEME.LY Create social videos with subtitles
(FREE)

ANIMAKER Make DIY animated videos in the cloud
($12/mo+)

INTOLIVE (iOS only) – Bring your photos to life with video
(FREE - $1.99)

ARROW Create videos with Augmented Reality graphics & emojis
(FREE)

QUIK From GoPro – edit videos on the go
(FREE)

FLYR Create professional looking Stories with interactive elements
(FREE-$2.99/mo+)

WEBSITE RESOURCES

WIX.COM Build a website without any coding skills
(FREE - $11/mo +)

SQUARESPACE.COM All in one website builder and host
(FREE - $12/mo +)

ADOBE SPARK PAGE Create beautiful single page sites in a magazine style layout
(FREE - $9/mo)

KINGSUMO WordPress plug in designed to help you grow your email subscriber list through "viral" giveaways on your website
($19/mo)

KISSMETRICS.COM Heavy duty website analytics such as conversion tracking & engagement metrics
($500/mo)

WHICHTESTWON.COM A website dedicated to A/B testing
(FREE)

CLICKTOTWEET.COM Help promote your content with this easy click to tweet link generator
(FREE)

ADDTHIS.COM/SHARETHIS.COM Help website visitors share your content with the click of a button
(FREE)

SNIP.LY Add a custom call to action button on any web page
($29/mo+)

ZENDESK CHAT Reach your customers via live chat on web, mobile and messaging platforms
($14/mo+)

BITLY.COM Create trackable URLs, shorten long links and create your own custom links
(FREE-$29/mo)

PRETTYLINKS.COM Create totally readable, easily speakable, and exceptionally memorable short links using your WordPress-based website and domain name
($59/mo)

UNBOUNCE.COM Affordable templated and customizable landing pages
($79/mo+)

MOBILE FRIENDLY TEST (GOOGLE) Google this term and find Google's free site that will tell you if your website is mobile friendly (and if it's not, it should be)
Search.google.com/test.mobile-friendly

EMAIL RESOURCES

SANEBOX.COM Clean up your email inbox
($7/mo+)

UNROLL.ME Unsubscribe from emails instantly
(FREE)

BOOMERANG Like a snooze button for your emails
(FREE-$4.99/mo+)

WISESTAMP.COM Custom email signatures with clickable social links
(FREE - $6/mo)

BOMBBOMB.COM Send video emails & texts to your database
($49/mo+)

CONVERTKIT Simple email sales funnel system to help convert website visitors
($29/mo+)

GENERAL RESOURCES

HITEMUPAPP.COM
Send personalized mass texts
(IOS only $2.50+)

WETRANSFER.COM Transfer very large files (up to 2GB) that cannot be emailed
(FREE)

MOO.COM Create incredible and unique business cards that people won't throw away
(Pricing Varies)

PDFESCAPE.COM Edit any pdf without Adobe
(FREE)

SLIDO An audience interaction tool for meetings, events and conferences. It offers interactive Q&A, live polls and insights about your audience
($199/event)

GOOGLE SLIDES/SHEETS/DRIVE/ FORMS An integrated suite of secure, cloud-native collaboration and productivity apps powered by google ai. includes gmail, docs, drive, calendar, meet and more.
(FREE)

GOOGLE DOCS VOICE DICTATION FEATURE
Automated voice typing within your Google doc – simply activate and start talking
(FREE)

DROPBOX.COM
Cloud storage for all of your files that allows you to share with others
(FREE - $8/mo+)

CALENDLY.COM
Stop emailing back and forth to find a meeting time – simple, easy to use scheduling system
(FREE - $8/mo+)

STATISTA.COM
Every stat you ever wanted complete with visual charts for presentations
(FREE - $49/mo+)

LASTPASS.COM
Password manager & digital wallet that allows others to log into your platforms without sharing your log in credentials
(FREE - $6/mo)

PDF2JPEG.NET
Turn any pdf document into a JPEG without downloading software
(FREE)

REFLECTOR DIRECTOR (AIRSQUIRRELS.COM)
Mirror your phone screen for a live presentation
($6.99)

SLACK APP
Real time messaging, file sharing and powerful search collaboration tool for teams like group text on steroids
(FREE)

ZAPIER.COM
Automate and connect multiple apps and platforms i.e. automate your Facebook leads to be automatically added to your CRM
(FREE - $20/mo+)

ALTERNATIVETO.NET
Find crowd sourced alternatives to software and tech
(FREE)

KAJABI.COM
Create, launch and sell your online courses
($149/mo+)

KEYWORD.IO
Advanced keyword research for your blog or YouTube video SEO
(FREE)

GOOGLE KEYWORD PLANNER
Advanced keyword research for your blog or YouTube video SEO
(FREE)

PRINT FRIENDLY & PDF CHROME EXTENSION
Automatically make print friendly format for any PDF
(FREE)

SLYDIAL.COM
Automated mass voice messaging system
($2.95/mo+)

VOICE RESOURCES: PODCASTING / FLASH BRIEFINGS

BUZZSPROUT.COM Easy podcast hosting, syndication and tracking
(FREE - $12+/mo)

LIBSYN.COM One-stop solution for everything you need to start podcasting, get your podcast in Apple Podcasts and iTunes, and even turn your show into an App
(FREE - 5+/mo)

SOUNDUPNOW.COM Alexa Flash Briefing Host & Skill Developer
(Starting at $14/mo)

GARAGEBAND (MAC) Built in software for MAC products that allows users to create and edit music, podcasts and recorded audio of any kind.
(FREE)

AUDACITYTEAM.ORG (PC)
Record and edit voice or music files with this free, open source, downloadable software compatible with all operating systems.
(FREE)

ALEXA APP A companion to your Amazon Echo, Dot, Tap and Show for setup, remote control, and enhanced features. Use this app to set up your voice-enabled devices, listen to music, flash briefings and more.
(FREE)

VOICE MEMO APP Record voice memos/ podcasts/flash briefing content directly into your smartphone or tablet.
(FREE)

ANCHOR.FM/ ANCHOR APP
The easiest way to start a podcast. Anchor's mobile app, iPad app, and desktop platform make it easy to capture audio anywhere, anytime
(FREE)

ALEXAFLASHBRIEFING.COM
Search for Alexa Flash Briefings from around the Universe – also, sign up to have your Flash Briefing included in this directory
(FREE)

INDUSTRYSYNDICATE.COM
The first real estate industry media company featuring top podcasts, flash briefings and live streams from all areas of real estate
(FREE)

YETI MICROPHONE
Premium USB and XLR microphones, and audiophile headphones for recording
(Amazon $110+)

BLUE SNOWBALL MIC
High quality microphone for top notch audio quality with USB connection.
(Amazon $49+)

RODE VIDEOMIC GO FOR SMARTPHONE
Plugs into your smartphone for on the go professional sound
(Amazon $60+)

ZAXSOUND CARDIOD CONDENSER MIC On the go with your podcast interviews? This portable mic will work with smartphones, laptops and tablets to record higher quality audio
(Amazon $25+)

MONOPRICE DESKTOP SOUNDBOOTH Improve your podcast audio quality by eliminating background noise with this mobile noise reducing booth
(Amazon $65+)

POP FILTER FOR MIC Reduces the harsh syllable sounds made when speaking and attaches to microphone
(Amazon $10+)

REPURPOSE.IO Repurpose your voice content into YouTube or Facebook videos and automatically publish them
($12/mo+)

HEADLINER.APP Turn your audio clip into a social media video post with sound
(FREE)

FIVERR.COM From logos to professionally voiced podcast intros, choose from a variety of virtual designers ranging in prices
(From $5 and up)

ZOOM.US For recording interviews with guests for your podcasts
(FREE- $14.99/mo+)

FREESOUND.ORG
Access a sound clip library for editing into your audio files
(FREE)

TEMI.COM OR SONIX.AI
Transcribe your podcast audio into text for repurposing to other platforms and formats
($0.10-$1/min)

PREMIUMBEAT.COM
Curated royalty-free music library by genre or mood ideal for video projects or podcast intros/outros.
($49 per license)

DAILY CONTENT PLANNER

MONDAY:

FORMAT:	TOPIC:	WHICH "E":
(f) Facebook Live Video	Veteran loan programs explained	Educational
(instagram)		
(in)		
(twitter)		
(youtube)		

Add your own additional platforms below:

(W) Website Blog Post	5 reasons to move to Boise	Educational
( )		

Comments:
💬 #

Shares/Shout outs / Tags:
➡ #

What worked?

Direct Messages:
✉ #

Connections added:
👥 #

TUESDAY:

FORMAT:	TOPIC:	WHICH "E":

f
_____

Instagram
_____

in
_____

Twitter
_____

YouTube
_____

Add your own additional platforms below:
_____

◯
_____

◯
_____

Comments:
💬 #
_____

Direct Messages:
✉ #
_____

Shares/Shout outs / Tags:
➥ #
_____

Connections added:
👥 #
_____

What worked?
_____
_____

WEDNESDAY:

FORMAT:	TOPIC:	WHICH "E":
(f)		
(Instagram)		
(in)		
(Twitter)		
(YouTube)		

Add your own additional platforms below:

◯

◯

Comments:	Shares/Shout outs / Tags:	What worked?
🗨 #	➡ #	
Direct Messages:	Connections added:	
✉ #	👥 #	

THURSDAY:

FORMAT:	TOPIC:	WHICH "E":

f

(Instagram)

(in)

(Twitter)

(YouTube)

Add your own additional platforms below:

◯

◯

Comments:	Shares/Shout outs / Tags:	What worked?
💬 #	➤ #	
Direct Messages:	Connections added:	
✉ #	👥 #	

FRIDAY:

FORMAT:	TOPIC:	WHICH "E":
f		
(instagram)		
(in)		
(twitter)		
(youtube)		

Add your own additional platforms below:

◯

◯

Comments:	Shares/Shout outs / Tags:	What worked?
🗨 #	➡ #	
Direct Messages:	Connections added:	
✉ #	👥 #	

SATURDAY:

FORMAT:	TOPIC:	WHICH "E":

(f) ....

(Instagram) ....

(in) ....

(twitter) ....

(youtube) ....

Add your own additional platforms below:

◯ ....

◯ ....

Comments:	Shares/Shout outs / Tags:	What worked?
💬 #	➡ #	
Direct Messages:	Connections added:	
✉ #	👥 #	

SUNDAY:

FORMAT:	TOPIC:	WHICH "E":
(f)		
(Instagram)		
(in)		
(Twitter)		
(YouTube)		

Add your own additional platforms below:

( )

( )

Comments:
🗨 #
....

Direct Messages:
✉ #
....

Shares/Shout outs / Tags:
➡ #
....

Connections added:
👥 #
....

What worked?
....
....
....

THE DO'S AND DON'TS OF CONTENT & SOCIAL MEDIA

CONTENT FAQ'S

How do I meaningfully engage with people on social media?

- In Jan 2018, Facebook announced a major change to its algorithm that would heavily weight comments.

  They stated that their goal was to encourage more "Meaningful Social Interactions" or engagement. This means that the algorithm assigns more value to posts that receive more interaction in the form of comments.

  When Facebook deems something "valuable," they will show that piece of content to more people and may also rank future content higher from the same person. Think of it this way- if you work with someone who has been reliable in the past, you're likely to give them more projects to work on in the future based on your previous experiences.

  This is why it's important to focus on quality content over quantity! It also means that your priority should be to make comments on your prospects' and clients' posts to stay top of mind!

- Stay efficient and intentional with your time and comments by setting up free customized "Friends Lists" within Facebook. You can create lists of homebuyers, sellers, past clients, prospects etc. Once the lists are set up, clicking on them will pull up a new feed that contains ONLY posts from those people. There's no searching for their posts, no chance of missing any of their posts and it saves you a ton of time scrolling through the feed. It becomes easy to stay top of mind through engaging comments.

- Time block your 'social prospecting' – engaging, commenting and sharing. It's important to spend 5-10 min BOTH in the morning and evening engaging with your community because there is so much content in the feed that most of your posts or comments are fairly shortlived. Think of this as "social prospecting" time.

- Stop the quick hitter likes, reactions and hearts. Those are what I call "social short cuts" and they make you feel good but don't really provide value (or build brand) for the creator.

  Facebook (and the person who posted) puts much more weight on long form comments vs. a quick like or emoji. The longer the comment, the more it shows Facebook that you care about that content.

- Highlight others. If you know someone who has achieved a goal, spoken at an event, written an article etc. share their post/content and include a heartfelt shout out as to why you are inspired by their efforts. Taking the time to share or talk about someone else's content shows that you care.

Do I have to be active on all the social networks?

NO.

As a general rule of thumb, go where your ideal customer is hanging out! (That said, don't be too sure that your ideal audience isn't using Instagram Stories or even Tik Tok)

It's absolutely okay to focus on one platform at a time.

Yes, every Social has its own 'flavor' or style (LinkedIn leans more professional, Instagram more relaxed and creative) but forcing yourself to be active on all of them can feel overwhelming. If you prefer one over another, then go all in on that one because anything you enjoy doing will seem less like a job.

Should I have the same username on all platforms?

Owning your name is important and creating a personal brand using that name matters. We Google everyone and everything. The Social Stalk is real and we do it because we can. It's not imperative to have the *exact* same username on all The Socials, but it certainly does help brand cohesiveness and also ease of following a brand on multiple platforms.

I heard organic reach is dead on (Platform Name) - is that true?

NO.

Organic (free) reach isn't what it used to be on saturated platforms like Facebook and Instagram, but that doesn't mean it's not possible. It does mean that your content will need to be interesting and valuable to a specific audience.

It also means that less crowded or newer platforms like Tik Tok could provide an opportunity to gain more free reach (for a while until they also become saturated).

If you want to go 'viral', I can't help you there. If I had a fail proof formula for viral content and could guarantee anyone could replicate it, I'd be very rich. Maybe that's my third book?

I heard that only teens are on (platform name) – why should I use it?

It's fairly rare for a mainstream social media platform to 'only' cater to a specific demographic for too long. It's common that platforms that originally skewed younger 'age up' over time. What we do know for certain is that it's users will!

Facebook started out as a site for college kids and now it's often considered the place where "parents hang out."

Things change. Fast and often.
This doesn't mean that you need to dive into every new app on the block, but the ones that make some waves shouldn't be ignored.

Consider the potential wins you could gain from test driving a new platform. What can you take away from a newer platform? Can you learn new video creation skills? Can you become more creative? Can you connect with your children through it?"

How much time do I need to spend each day on The Socials?

In the beginning, it's going to take you more time to learn any new platform or feature. Learning to edit a video for an IGTV post for the first time could take 30-60 minutes. As you become more accustomed to the platforms and how to use them, your time is more efficiently spent.

Aim for 10-15 minutes in the morning and at night engaging with others on the platforms through comments and direct messages. Crafting higher quality content will take a bit more time but remember, you're posting less often. This too will become easier and faster with practice. Pre-planning your content and time-blocking can help you become more efficient and strategic.

How often should I post?

The algorithms are rewarding quality over quantity. Because Facebook and Instagram are very saturated with high levels of daily users, the content flowing through the Feeds can become overwhelming.

When your content receives higher engagement, it will perform better and get more free reach.

By focusing on creating higher quality content that will appeal to your audience you can work smarter, not harder and post 1-2 times per week and still maintain good reach.

In many cases, posting too frequently can negatively impact your reach and your content could even start competing with itself if you're posting multiple times a day.

'Feed fillers' AKA posts made for the sake of posting often don't get high engagement levels which can negatively impact your future reach. Spend your time focusing on commenting and sharing your target audience's content. Participating in conversations and becoming someone's "superfan" keeps your brand top of mind.

Does it matter what time of day I post?

Knowing when your audience is most active on a platform makes sense to maximize engagement. Typically, it's first thing in the morning, lunchtime and before bed. If you want to get more insights into your specific community's activity, check out the insights section of your Facebook Business Page or Instagram Business Account.

Keep in mind that you can absolutely schedule your posts around more active times or post in the moment when it suits you. The most important part of any post is your response to all of the comments! Never leave a comment behind! Always respond, not only because it's appropriate social etiquette but also because it's going to positively impact the algorithms on the platforms. They want to see that you are an engaged user!

My business is almost all by referral. Do I really need to use social media?

The average American spends upwards of 136 minutes per day on social media. This is where your community is posting birthdays, new babies and other important life events. It's the PERFECT place for you to stay in touch with your clients!

Social media is a peek into the life of your clients and an excellent way to communicate with them and stay top of mind.

Sending emails, newsletters or postcards still work (everything works with consistency). Imagine complimenting those physical marketing pieces with digital branding showing your face in a Feed where almost very potential client it scrolling through daily.

Should I completely separate my personal content from business content?

Human behavior is being changed by technology. We have access to unlimited amounts of data online and we have gotten used to seeing personal brands on social media.

From Instagram Stories to YouTube videos, we can tune in to anyone's realty tv channel. There's a time and place for business and personal content to be separate, but by and large, we can intertwine the two at some level.

Can you be uber successful with only sharing business content? Absolutely!

Will you be even more successful if you sprinkle in a little humanity? Probably.

Should I connect my Instagram and Facebook accounts (or other socials)?

Posting the same piece of content to multiple platforms at the same time is called cross-posting. Typically it's due to linking accounts or using a third party scheduling platform.

There may be instances in which you want to share that post everywhere at the same time (ex: launch or big announcement), however, keep in mind that your audience may be connected with you on more than one channel.

For example, if your friend posts the same content to both Instagram and Facebook Stories, you might stop viewing one of those channels assuming it's a repeat.

Additionally, there is platform-specific "lingo" that may not make sense when cross-posting. Hashtags are critical in any Instagram post, but not so on Facebook. It's a little unfair, but some people might even perceive cross-posting as 'lazy'.

An alternative approach is repurposing your content.

Repurposing content is a way to recycle a piece of content by changing its original format. Your Facebook live video could become a blog post or podcast. Your YouTube video could become a new IGTV series of micro videos.

Editing and reformatting content is a smart way to squeeze more juice out of your content.

What's the perfect video length?

There isn't one. Many people have experienced massive success with a 6 second video as well as a 60 minute video.

Your goal should be:
- Start making videos
- Get consistent
- Get comfortable
- Get better

Once you have become more comfortable in front of the camera THEN and only then should you aim to increase your length, hooks, calls to action and watch time.

Facebook is watching for videos with 3+ minutes and 1+ minute of watch time as well as return viewers.

3 minutes of a bad video is still 3 minutes of a bad video that no one will watch. Don't let these guidelines intimidate you! Create a video of ANY length to get started and keep going!

Should I post vertical or horizontal video?

Many platforms have embraced vertical videos because we naturally hold our phones in that position while scrolling and viewing. Facebook Stories, Instagram Stories, Tik Tok,

Snapchat and IGTV were made for full screen vertical viewing.

Vertical videos also take up more space in Facebook and LinkedIn Feeds which grabs attention, increases views and engagement.

Don't count horizontal videos out! Any video with valuable content works! If you're posting to YouTube, horizontal video is the norm. If you are creating horizontal video and want to repurpose into a vertical format, check out the InShot app or any video resizing app.

Maybe the best answer is...both.

I don't like watching Facebook Live videos, why would I ever make one?

Yes, its true, some of us do not prefer to watch a Live video on Facebook. My suggestion is to consider two concepts:

1. Facebook rewards users who go live by showing that post to more people which means your brand awareness will increase over time as your target audience sees your face over and over again in the feed. It's one of the most effective ways to increase reach for free on Facebook.

Even if people don't watch your broadcasts or only watch a portion, they will still see your face.

2. It's not about your preferences. We may prefer to email while our potential clients prefer to text message or talk on the phone.

Keep in mind that as behaviors are trained

towards video through social platforms and apps we use daily outside of Real Estate, more and more people are in fact watching video included live broadcasts. (If you prefer not to create a live broadcast, consider creating a recorded video and uploading to Facebook or creating a YouTube channel, using Instagram Stories or even Snapchat for alternative video based options).

Facebook reports that live videos receive 6x more engagement than any other form of content posted. Part of that is due to their algorithms and part of it is due to seeing your FACE and being able to talk with you live!

I've been doing live video and social posts for a few weeks why isn't it working?

Brand awareness is not just about creating and sharing your message. It's primarily about the consistency and the frequency with which you share that message. It's critical that you implement the following best practices to grow your reach, brand and community:

- Create a consistent schedule for content creation, research and posting

- Thoughtfully comment and engage with your target audience on a daily basis

- Add captions to your videos to increase engagement and provide context

- Analyze your insights – when are viewers dropping off? Can you improve your intro, hook and calls to action?

In the end, it's mostly about staying the course with your own content creation and posting and being patient! Think of it this way, would you expect to list several homes after mailing one postcard to someone's home?

What's a "good" engagement rate?

This is hard to answer with exactness. Many sources report that the following ranges as industry benchmarks:

- Less than 1% = low engagement rate
- Between 1% and 3.5% = average/good engagement rate
- Between 3.5% and 6% = high engagement rate
- Above 6% = very high engagement rate

The formula to determine your engagement rate is :

Likes + comments (divided by) Follower count

You can check your in app insights and analytics on a weekly basis or a per post basis over several months with a good ol fashioned spreadsheet and look for increases or decreases.

There are many paid third party tools that will provide you with reports as well.

Should I pay for social media ads?

Paid advertising is an excellent way to get your content in front of your ideal audience. Social media ads generally can be less expensive than many other forms of advertising and are served where the majority of the population is spending their time and attention.

Depending on the ad image, copy and targeting, your ad could generate leads that are ready to act immediately or that will need to be nurtured over time and receive multiple touch points before converting.

If I use a third party content scheduler, will that negatively impact the algorithms?

According to many research reports, third party social media content schedulers do not negatively impact your algorithm. Years ago, that may have been the case, but currently many social media marketers and content creators successfully use these platforms to post and analyze data points.
Check out a list of approved vendor partners here: www.facebook.com/business/partner-directory

I heard about a system that's affordable that will do the posting for me- should I use it?

There are many services available that will post to your social on your behalf or provide you with content to copy and paste.

While this may sound like a time saver, it also typically is generic content that is very likely being used for other people as well. This kind of content may not generate the kind of engagement you are hoping for.

If you are posting and no one is engaging, then most platforms' algorithms will likely down-rank all of your content because no one is showing interest.

Social is the key word in Social Media and that means you can't outsource being human.

Can I totally outsource my content?

Yes, you can, but there are some important things to remember if you do!

If you're considering hiring an agency, copywriter or marketing team member, be sure to complete your due diligence. Spend time with them to ensure that they understand your message and deliver it in your desired brand voice.

Is outsourcing a lot easier? Sure is.
More expensive? Yep.
Worth it? Can't answer that for you.

While you can outsource content creation, what you can't easily outsource is your personal brand. The consumer expects to see your brand online and engage with it easily.

Does Follower count matter?

NO.

If you are attempting to land a paid gig as an "influencer" then maybe.

Otherwise, focus on going deeper with your community before you go wider. Think about this – if you have 20 people watch your Instagram Story, that's 20 human beings that consumed your content and brand – can you meet with 20 people in a day?

Should I follow everyone who follows me?

Ultimately, you decide who to follow/follow back and why.

When considering following someone's account, ask yourself, "is this someone who I think is interesting? Inspiring? Entertaining? In my industry?"

Will some people feel offended if you don't reciprocate? Sure, but that's on them, not you.

I've been contacted by a company that says they can get me real followers and engagement- should I do it?

HARD NO.

Every Social has software that is "smart" enough to know if you suddenly skyrocket your follower count or if your account is being logged into from different IP Addresses all over the globe.

Purchased follows, likes, views and comments will likely come from accounts that are not actually interested in using your services, let alone be 'real'. Additionally, if you have a high follower count but low engagement on your posts, the Socials know that something's up and the reach of your future content could be affected. You might get more engagement in the beginning that typically tapers off over time. Engagement is one of the major ways Instagram's algorithm determines your post's reach.

Additionally, they might be illegal based on a 2019 FTC ruling: *http://bit.ly/FTCFakeFollowers*

Can liking or commenting too quickly on content get me blocked?

YES.

The Socials have limitations to the number of actions that can be taken within a certain timeframe. They do this to spot and eliminate potential spammers and automated software systems.

For example, "liking" too many posts within a short amount of time or commenting too quickly one right after another could trigger the platform's software to block a user thinking that they could be a 'bot' or employing a third party automated software to take those spam-like actions.

Action blocks usually 24-72 hours and there's not too much a user can do other than wait it out.

**Also, simply using an app that connects to a Social that helps users see analytics or mass follow/unfollow can also result in an action block.

CHELSEA-ISMS

A list of phrases I say a lot that sum up this workbook...

- Faces take you places

- Less contenting, more commenting

- Don't stalk unless you talk

- Build trust through tech

- Frequency builds trust

- Teach before you reach

- Stories not sales pitches

- Value + Trust = Influence

- Algorithms + Content + Perceptions = Personal Brand

- I do what + for whom = that results in (UVP)

- Let your comments be your content

- Dialogues over data

- It's not a live stream, it's a life stream

- The camera is the new social feed

- I stopped watching television, because it doesn't talk back

- We're in an era of arm's-length communication

- Being you is 100% scalable

- Authenticity beats an algorithm every time

- There's magic in the mundane

- It's about communication, not commercials

- Relatability is the most underleveraged marketing strategy today

- Industry is irrelevant, behavior is not

- Social isn't media

ABOUT THE AUTHOR

Chelsea Peitz is the National Director of Social Sales for Fidelity National Financial and a nationally recognized real estate keynote speaker who teaches sales professionals how to leverage social media and technology to build a powerful personal brand and develop content that generates real leads.

Chelsea is also the published author of the book, Talking in Pictures: How Snapchat Changed Communication, Cameras and Communities - the only book about how camera first social platforms have changed how we build a personal brand.

She's married to her soulmate, Brian, and mom to her mini-me, Mason. When not on The Socials, Chelsea loves a glass of a big bold cab, Netflixing her face off and listening to true crime podcasts.

THE WEBSITE:
ChelseaPeitz.com
(Don't email me, DM me on Insta!)

THE PODCAST:
The Voice of Social Sales
https://apple.co/2XrjmAG

THE SOCIALS:
Instagram: @chelsea.peitz
Facebook: facebook.com/chelschats
LinkedIn: www.linkedin.com/in/chelseapeitz/
Snapchat: @chelsea.peitz
TikTok: @chelsea.Peitz
YouTube: youtube.com/c/ChelseaPeitz

If you found value in this book or the content I provide, please consider leaving a review on Amazon, it really helps this content get more reach!

DON'T FORGET to spread the word by posting about this book and tagging me in it! Thank you in advance!

ADDITIONAL RESOURCES

Additional resources for content included and/or referenced in this book:

Pgs 28-29: Core Values Words https://scottjeffrey.com/core-values-list/

Pg 34: Positive Action Verbs https://boompositive.com/pages/list-of-positive-verbs-a-to-z

Pg 47: Gary Vaynerchuk's Context tips: www.garyvaynerchuk.com/content-is-king-but-context-is-god

Pg 123: Quote Copyblogger:

Pgs 124-126: Buzzsumo article about headlines: https://buzzsumo.com/blog/most-shared-headlines-study/

Pgs 127-129 Hook starters: https://bid4papers.com/blog/hook-for-essay/

Pg 131: 180+ power words list: https://www.slideshare.net/coschedule/180-words-to-use

Pg 132: 12 most influential words: https://www.slideshare.net/06021954/12-most-powerful-words-in-english

https://copyblogger.com/persuasive-copywriting-words/

http://itre.cis.upenn.edu/~myl/languagelog/archives/003659.html

Pages 136- 139 Copywriting Formulas:
https://buffer.com/resources/copywriting-formulas

Pg 140-141: AIDA example and ad example: Travis Thom travisthom.com Elevated Real Estate Marketing: http://www.travisthom.com/
https://www.facebook.com/groups/leads2listingmasterminds/

Pg 142 Call to action examples: https://blog.hubspot.com/marketing/call-to-action-examples

Pg 151: Buffer article on Facebook algorithm updates:

https://buffer.com/library/facebook-news-feed-algorithm

https://buffer.com/resources/facebook-algorithm

Pg 156: Trish Leto, Creator of 5 Minute Lives™ and Press Live with Purpose™ shares her outline for live video formatting: https://podcasts.apple.com/us/podcast/ep-19-facebook-live-video-ninja-tips-with-trish-leto/id1345633548?i=1000434361265&l=fr

Pg 164: SocialInsider.io article: https://www.socialinsider.io/blog/facebook-video-study/

Pg 166: 6 Factors of Instagram Algorithm: https://techcrunch.com/2018/06/01/how-instagram-feed-works/

Pg. 167: TechCrunch Instagram algorithm article: https://techcrunch.com/2018/06/01/how-instagram-feed-works/

Pg 176: 85% of video content watched without sound: https://www.niemanlab.org/reading/publishers-say-85-percent-of-facebook-video-is-watched-without-sound/

Pg 176: 80% quote from CoVideo.com: https://www.covideo.com/why-you-need-to-add-captions-to-your-videos-now

Pg 179: Optimal Foraging Theory info: https://www.sparknotes.com/biology/animalbehavior/behavioralecology/section1/

Pg 187: Native Content: https://www.forbes.com/sites/johnkoetsier/2017/03/13/facebook-native-video-gets-10x-more-shares-than-youtube/#55c437041c66

Pg 191: 3.5 Billion Google searches per day: https://www.internetlivestats.com/google-search-statistics/

Pg 193: Domo.com infographic regarding what happens in 60 seconds online in 2019: https://www.digitalinformationworld.com/2019/07/data-never-sleeps-7-infographic.html

Pg 193: Mark Zuckerberg's quote about Stories as the future: https://www.cnbc.com/2018/10/30/mark-zuckerberg-q318-earnings-call-how-facebook-is-changing.html

Pgs 201-216 Insights Explanations and Creator Studio images:

https://www.facebook.com/business/learn/lessons/creator-studio-overview

https://www.facebook.com/help/publisher/manage/about-facebook-creator-studio

Pg 213 Images sourced from Later.com blog post

Pg 243 The average American spends upwards of 136 minutes per day on social media: https://www.statista.com/statistics/433871/daily-social-media-usage-worldwide/

Pg 245 Industry benchmark "good" engagement rates: There are multiple resources for these benchmarks – here's the blog I sourced from: https://www.scrunch.com/blog/what-is-a-good-engagement-rate-on-instagram

Made in United States
Orlando, FL
23 July 2023

35387709R10137